THE SOCIALISM OF FOOLS
Anti-Semitism on the Left

Michael Lerner

TIKKUN BOOKS

Published by TIKKUN BOOKS

5100 Leona Street
Oakland, CA 94619

P.O. Box 10528
Jerusalem, Israel 91103

Printed in the United States of America

Library of Congress Cataloging-in-Publication Data
Lerner, Michael
The Socialism of Fools: Anti-Semitism on the Left

Library of Congress Catalogue Number: 91-067800

ISBN: 0-935933-05-0

Contents

iii

In loving memory of my mother,
Beatrice Irene Hirschman Lerner

Preface

This book is not written just for people who identify with the Left or with activists in liberal and progressive social-change movements. The ideas that are being confronted here can be found throughout the educated sectors of Western society, and the anti-Semitism that I describe is often an ingredient in the consciousness of many people who think of themselves as beyond politics, uninterested in social issues, or not even willing to acknowledge that they think about others in terms of religious, cultural, ethnic, or national backgrounds. Indeed, it is all too easy for people to think of the Left in narrow terms, as those who hold some specific radical ideology. But the Left I am addressing is the broad intellectual and cultural Left, which includes people who never intend to be involved in political struggle but who share with the political Left the sensibility that there is something not OK about the way things are, oppose racism, patriarchy, and militarism, and are generally sympathetic to using government power to eliminate poverty and inequality and to constrain corporate abuse of the environment. In the contemporary period, that sensibility is often articulated in a form of cynicism and pessimism that is deeply skeptical about the possibility of changing things, and hence deeply skeptical about current social-change movements. This book is targeted as much at the skeptics and cynics as at those who make up the more narrowly defined Left.

The main danger to the Jewish people is *not* now, nor has it ever been, from the Left. The Right is always the main threat. Even if the whole language of "Left" and "Right" seems dated and unable to embody the complexities of politics in the 1990s, the historical tendency of the Right will remain a force: the tendency to defend the established distribution of wealth and power and to see that distribution as fundamentally just.

From the standpoint of the Right, Jews will always be a threat, for reasons that I shall describe below. To the extent that the Jewish people continue to tell their own liberation story, and continue to see that as the center of their religious and cultural life, the message must always remain a challenge to those who seek to justify existing class injustice. For that reason, the Right will have a motivation to make Jews into "the enemy," at least to the extent that the Jews remain connected to their fundamentally revolutionary message. And one way that the Right can deal with the frustration of others who are oppressed is to direct their anger at the Jews.

The special oppression of Jews is that they are not typically placed in the same position as the rest of the oppressed, but often have the "opportunity" to serve ruling interests by being placed in an intermediary position between the oppressed and the oppressors. Often they appear to the oppressed as the public faces of the oppressor. This special position of vulnerability is the specific nature of Jewish oppression. And it is this specific form of oppression that then leads to the frequently actualized possibility that when the masses become angry at oppression, they direct that anger at the Jews instead of at the ruling classes. This is what August Bebel called "the socialism of fools."

The tragic irony of the past hundred years is that those who have been involved in the liberal and progressive social-change movements, instead of realizing that they must systematically unmask this "socialism of fools" and redirect anger at those with real power, have instead sometimes acquiesced to and even participated in the very belief structures that make anti-Semitism popular. And while anti-Semitism on the Left today tends to be unconscious, it has a long history of not always being unconscious or unwitting.

The Left's failure to confront this socialism of fools, and its complicity in the long Western tradition of denigrating the Jews, is a tremendous moral and political disgrace. But it is not an indictment of the fundamental moral and political commitments of the liberal and progressive social-change movements, any more than the severe manifestations of sexism and chauvinism in some aspects of Jewish traditional observances are compelling reasons to give up on the fundamentally liberatory ideas of Judaism, or the distortions that have taken place in the practice of psychoanalysts or in the history of women's movements good reasons to give up on the liberatory elements in these traditions. The discussion presented in this book is not aimed at supporting right-wing conclusions. That the Left as a social movement has been fundamentally flawed by monumental insensitivity, and at times overt Jew-hating, does not necessarily invalidate the Left critique of capitalist society or make one want to abandon the Left's egalitarian and democratic impulses. Here, as in the history of the Jewish people, we must accept the fact that human beings have inherited a legacy of pain that inevitably distorts us and makes us less than we can and ought to be. It is with much compassion for the Left that I present this analysis, and with the hopes that people on the Left will recognize, after reading this book, that the movement to transform this society will be stronger and healthier once it has committed itself to eliminating all vestiges of anti-Semitism.

I have not attempted a scholarly presentation or detailed proof of the position being presented here. I have drawn on the research of others, but have not attempted to cite all sources or prove historical facts. Rather, this is an interpretive essay that attempts to show how the various facts cohere, and what they mean from the standpoint of someone with what is sometimes called a "Jewish liberation" or "Jewish renewal" perspective. I am not attempting to present new information, but rather a morally coherent ordering of information that is already widely known but rarely put together in a fashion that addresses people with a contemporary progressive consciousness. Aspects of the interpretation of a given historical epic might be questioned by later scholars—but I believe that even when we take into account all the specifics that might be contested, the overall framework stands as a significant moral challenge, not only to social change activists, but to many progressive intellectuals and creators of culture in the West who have never seriously thought about the issues raised herein. Those who wish to avoid that challenge may focus on a detail here or there; but they would better serve the cause of liberation and intellectual honesty if they were to confront the fundamental perspective that demonstrates a wild level of insensitivity to Jewish questions on the Left and a (sometimes unconscious) participation in anti-Semitic ideas and practices. And this same insensitivity extends through much of Western culture and even finds expression in the thinking and writing of Jewish intellectuals who have become important participants and shapers of this larger cultural arena.

A cautionary note about my interpretation of Judaism and Jewish history: I am well aware that it is only one possible interpretation, and there are many in the Jewish world who will contend against it. In a forthcoming book on Jewish liberation theology and its relevance to contemporary movements for social change, I will make a fuller defense of my interpretation. The texts and the facts do not speak for themselves—we always deal with some particular selection of facts and texts and some particular reading of those that have been selected. Reading this book will give the reader some hints of why I believe that Judaism and Jewish history have something important to teach contemporary progressive intellectuals, whether Jewish or not. Some of those hints are developed more fully in my articles in *Tikkun* and the *Tikkun Anthology,* but the full articulation will have to await my book on Jewish theology.

Introduction

I decided to write this book in response to hundreds of calls and letters that we received at *Tikkun* magazine from readers who reported incidents of anti-Semitism in the various social-change movements in which they participated.

Here are a few of the reports we received:

- A student at the University of California, Santa Cruz, reported that Uhuru House, an African-American group, sponsored a speaker who talked about Jews "controlling the media." At a subsequent rally a speaker said, "Israel should be destroyed and anyone who thinks otherwise is part of the imperialist capitalist system."

- A student at Barnard College reported that when Jews on the student council raised objections to the appearance of Professor Griff, a former member of the rap group Public Enemy, on the grounds of what they perceived to be his anti-Semitic, sexist, and homophobic language, they were greeted with comments such as "too bad Hitler didn't finish the job." When another Barnard student urged the feminist group she was part of to take a stand against Griff, she was told that the group would support action against Griff only if he made sexist and homophobic statements in his speech on campus; anti-Semitic statements alone were not enough to warrant action.

• Todd Gitlin, professor of sociology at the University of California, Berkeley and author of *The Sixties,* reported that in the early days of the Gulf War,

> a militant antiwar activist approached me on the Berkeley campus and started yelling at me that I shouldn't talk to the press unless an Arab professor was at my side. Another man, an African American, peppered the discussion with taunts: "You brought me here!" "You profit from my being brought here!" Finally: "Read Henry Ford, *The International Jew!*" Horrified, I said that was Nazi propaganda, garbage. Naively, I had trouble believing that the flagrant, loathsome, anti-Semitic propaganda of a half-century ago was back in circulation.

> Two days later, at the invitation of an African American colleague, I went to a meeting called by an African American student ostensibly to hash out Jewish-Black differences. There, a representative of a Muslim organization called the Gulf War "a Jewish war" because, he maintained, "there are two Jews in Congress and both of them support the war," and because Henry Kissinger supported the war and Henry Kissinger was well-known for his support of Israel. I interrupted to say that there were, in fact, twenty-eight Jews in Congress and that a majority of them had opposed the war; and moreover, that Henry Kissinger did not speak for Jews in general. There ensued a dispute on the less-than-burning question of the exact number of Jews in Congress. I was appalled that none of the non-Jews present, faculty or students, intervened to say that to dispute the precise number was to miss the point. One African American colleague did say at the end of the meeting that the great unconfronted issue of the day was Israeli arms sales to Central America.

> The next day, January 26, at the antiwar rally in San Francisco, I was telling this story to a friend, who told me about a friend of his, a longtime environmental activist, who had recently said to him: "I finally read something that explains to me what's going on in the world." When my friend inquired about what it was, he was told, "A pamphlet called *Protocols of the Elders of Zion.*"

• Another professor at the University of California, Berkeley, Barbara Epstein, reported feeling that Gitlin was "exaggerating" when he first reported these incidents. She changed her mind after a subsequent antiwar forum in which the first questioner asked, "Why are Jews trying to run the world?" Epstein was struck not by the question itself, but by the willingness of the audience to listen to statements that, if made about any other group, would have provoked an immediate uproar of dissent and anger.

- At a Boston teach-in on the Gulf War, someone who identified himself as associated with the leftist magazine *Z* said that he was "disgusted" with the Jewish reaction to the war. The Jews, he claimed, were making a big fuss about the SCUDs falling on Israel but were simultaneously ignoring the pain of the Iraqis who were being killed. A participant asked others in the room if they could imagine anyone saying that they were disgusted if the country attacked by SCUDs had been a country in Africa and African Americans had shown more concern about that country than about the fate of the Iraqis. The participant was immediately denounced as "a narrow-minded Zionist."

Karen Abrams, working as a research assistant for *Tikkun,* collected many such stories and experiences from all parts of the country. It became clear to us that there was a general problem that could neither be dismissed nor ignored.

There have been other books about anti-Semitism on the Left. Yet most of them have been written by people connected to the American Jewish establishment who are fundamentally hostile to the Left's agenda, and who are attempting to use the fact of anti-Semitism to discredit the Left and credit themselves or their organizations as loyal members of the American political mainstream. This book has no such agenda. It is produced by the Committee for Judaism and Social Justice, the education arm of *Tikkun.* Our purpose in raising these issues is to strengthen the liberal and progressive social-change movements by helping them confront and eliminate a major problem within their ranks.

From our perspective, *tikkun olam,* the transformation of the world into a more just, peaceful, and nurturing place, is a central injunction of the Jewish tradition. In that sense, we believe that Jews ought to be committed to the liberal and progressive social-change movements. Yet those movements are also deeply flawed, and one of the important dimensions of those flaws is connected to the way they deal with Jews.

Our critique emanates not from the desire to hurt or undermine, but to repair and strengthen the movements for peace, justice, feminism, gay and lesbian liberation, Black liberation, human rights, environmental sanity, and all the other important liberal and progressive social-change activities of the 1990s. We believe that the Right poses a far greater threat to the well-being of Jews than the Left.

It is the Right's anti-Semitism, not that of the Left, that would be more likely to lead to actual repression of and danger to Jews. It is in the interest of Jews that liberal and progressive social-change movements succeed and flourish. And it is precisely for that reason that Jews must combat the anti-Semitism within these movements. If you are an activist in any of these social-change movements, we hope you will read this material and share it with your friends and colleagues.

Yet this is also meant for Jewish students on campus and for Jews in social-change organizations who experience a latent or sometimes overt hostility from some activists on the Left. This book should help them learn how to recognize the difference between legitimate and anti-Semitic criticisms of Jews or Israel. At the same time, it should be useful to them to help non-Jews in progressive movements understand why some Jews who might otherwise be an active part of social-change movements get turned off by what they often correctly perceive to be a tinge of hostility toward Jews.

Research for this book was funded in part by the Nathan Cummings Foundation. Special thanks to Karen Abrams for research assistance, to David Stein for copy editing help, and to Wendy Orange for her support.

Research for this book was also funded by the Manfred and Anne Lehmann Foundation. The Lehmann Foundation, however, does not endorse all of the premises and conclusions of the author.

If the ideas in this book help you, excite you, or energize you, help us get them better circulation. Get others to buy and read this book, to subscribe to *Tikkun,* to purchase the *Tikkun Anthology,* and to become active in *Tikkun*'s education/outreach organization, the Committee for Judaism and Social Justice (CJSJ), or its youth arm, Students for Judaism and Social Justice (SJSJ).

1

What is Anti-Semitism?

Hatred of Jews is the oldest and most continuous form of racism in the Western and Islamic worlds. It is so deeply embedded in the assumptions and thought patterns of the West that some of the most "enlightened" writers and thinkers, social-change activists and humanitarians unconsciously embody and articulate anti-Semitic attitudes and ideas.

For our purposes, anti-Semitism is the systematic discrimination against, denigration, or oppression of Jews, Judaism, and the cultural, intellectual, and religious heritage of the Jewish people.

Anti-Semitism can be overt and vicious, as in the case of Christianity's treatment of Jews through most of its two-thousand-year history, or it can be more subtle, as in the case of those who say that they don't really hate *all* Jews, but only Jews of a certain type (Jews who are religious, secular, wealthy, uneducated, in business, pushy, Zionist, etc.).

It can take the form of denying the documented realities of Jewish history (e.g., imagining that Jews did something *as a people* to warrant the oppression they faced, denying the oppression altogether, or denying that the Holocaust happened), or it can take the form of fantasizing that Jews are omnipresent and omnipotent—that Jews run the world or control everything.

Anti-Semitism can at times be a set of racist attitudes toward the Jewish people (the belief that they are somehow worse or more dangerous than others). But it can at other times be structural policies that have the effect of disproportionately and unfairly disadvantaging Jews (e.g., quotas in higher education or in professions that limit Jews to their actual proportion of the population as a whole).

As with other forms of racism, anti-Semitism does not require conscious intent. Just as people systematically devalue African Americans in ways that are completely unconscious and deeply ingrained in our culture, so one can honestly imagine that one "likes Jews" or has "a positive attitude" toward Jewishness and still have

1

anti-Semitic attitudes and actions embedded in one's thinking, speech, and behavior.

Though the phenomenon has a long history, use of the word "anti-Semitism" to cover the complex set of Jew-hating phenomena in the Western world emerged only in the nineteenth century, under the influence of intellectuals who were beginning to divide the world according to race. In fact, there is little reason to believe that there are any acceptable definitions of "race" that refer solely to physical or biological phenomena. The whole notion of race is itself racist. It derives from and reinforces notions that certain groups of people, defined in terms of inherent physical characteristics, deserve to be treated differently from others.

If race were defined in physical terms, it would be hard to argue that Jews share any particular set of physical characteristics. In Israel, for example, one finds black Jews from Ethiopia who seem much more similar physically to their neighbors in Ethiopia than to Jews from Eastern Europe. Jews from Islamic lands look physically indistinguishable from many Arabs, and Jews from Europe look physically indistinguishable from many other Eastern and Central Europeans. So calling Jews a "race" of Semites is itself problematic, just as it is problematic to call Arabs a "race" of Semites.

Nevertheless, the term "anti-Semitism" was accepted in popular discourse as the general term for Jew-hating, and so we use it here in that sense.

Some Black nationalists have recently insisted that the Jews aren't "really" Semites and hence cannot be victims of anti-Semitism. This is patently absurd. On the one hand, as I've said, if "Semite" is a racial designation, the whole notion of race is problematic. If it's a description of a cultural heritage, there is little doubt that the Jewish cultural and religious heritage derives from our historical experience in the ancient middle east and could legitimately be called Semitic in that sense. But the more fundamental point is that the word anti-Semitism has come to refer to the practice of Jew-hating, and we Jews have accepted this term and have every right to pick the language we want as the label for the practice of oppressing or acting negatively toward Jews. Conversely, imagine how offensive it would be if Jews began to argue that there was no discrimination against African Americans because there really were no African Americans, since the Blacks in America have a different skin color and different historical characteristics from those who today live in Africa. This kind of nit-picking is merely a cover for hatred of one group by another.

2

Origins of the Anti-Semitic Pathology

Jews as Revolutionaries

From our earliest recorded history, the Jewish people have been the objects of both respect and hatred, admiration and fear. Non-Jewish intellectuals sometimes praised the Jews for their advanced concept of God and their highly developed legal and moral codes. On the other hand, those most closely aligned to the ruling elites of their society were often involved in calumny and denigration of Judaism and the Jewish people.

It is no wonder that ruling elites felt threatened by the Jewish people or hoped to foster a distance and provoke anger between the Jews and other peoples in the various empires of the ancient world. One need only pay attention to the *content* of Jewish religion to understand why ruling elites always hated the Jews.

Although the origins of the Jewish people were clouded in historical debate, the Jews emerged into history with a conception of themselves as a group who had been enslaved in Egypt, and who had subsequently broken out of slavery and created a free and self-governing existence for themselves in the area they called Judea and Israel.

Elites in the ancient world tended to rule through a combination of brute force and the imposition of various ideologies whose central theme was that existing class divisions were sanctified by an unchanging natural order. Whether in the form of ancient myths about the gods who ruled nature, or in the far more sophisticated

3

form proposed by Plato in *The Republic,* elite ideology destined society to remain divided by class, either by virtue of some inherent feature of each class itself or by the will of the gods.

Jewish existence was living testimony that these myths and ideologies were invented to perpetuate the needs and interests of the ruling class. Jews had managed to break out of the most degraded position on the class ladder, slavery, and had gone on to run their own society successfully. As long as the Jews existed, the ruling elites were wrong and their rule was in question.

Perhaps this fact about Jewish history might have been less threatening had Jews buried their story of origins in a few mythic tales that were rarely told. Instead, the entire Jewish religion was built upon retelling this story every week! The account of the liberation struggle was the main subject of the Torah, which was divided into fifty-two roughly equal sections. One section was read each week until the whole story was completed, and then the cycle would start again. The central Jewish observance, Shabbat, the Sabbath or day of rest, was to be observed "in commemoration of the exodus from Egypt" by setting aside one day per week when *no one* could make the Jews work. The very idea that the oppressed could set a limit on their oppression, and that the oppressors would have to kill them before they would work on that day, was itself a revolutionary reform—the first real victory in the class struggle against the oppressors and an enduring, weekly reminder that oppression could be overcome.

Even Judaism's essential concept of God is revolutionary. God described her/himself to Moses as *ehyeh asher ehyeh,* which means "I shall be whom I shall be"—that is, the primary force that rules the universe is the principle of freedom and possibility. Unlike the gods of nature, it is the force of possibility that rules the universe, and hence there is always the possibility that everything can be changed (including the entire social order of oppression).

Of course, as Jews settled into their land, were conquered by various imperial forces, and attempted to live within the framework of imperial rule in the ancient world, some of the revolutionary message of their religion fell away or was played down. Yet for many ruling elites, the revolutionary message was all too present in Judaism—in its egalitarian practices with regard to class, in its constant retelling of the story of the liberation from Egypt, and in its anti-authoritarian ethos (e.g., refusing to bow down to kings or rulers). And no matter how hard many individual Jews tried to de-emphasize these confrontational aspects of their religion, no matter how desperately individual Jews sought to make accommodations or identify themselves with the imperial powers and their dominant values, the collective memory of independence and freedom—preserved in the Jewish religion and manifest in the (often unconscious) way that Jews presented themselves as a group—made the Jews the most cantankerous people of the ancient world, the one group that rebelled against Hellenistic and then Roman rule with greater ferocity and frequency than any other.

I have no interest in romanticizing the realities of Jewish society or Judaism. Alongside the revolutionary ethos, and sometimes even within the very same people who expressed this revolutionary yearning, there remained deep ethical distortions. The sexism and xenophobia built into the religious practices, the willingness to claim a history of conquering the dwellers of Canaan (though historical scholarship has now cast grave doubts on whether such a conquest ever took place), the compromises with slavery, and the slaughter of the enemy (as detailed in Samuel's condemnation of Saul for not killing the Amalekite king)—all these were also part of the reality of ancient Israel. It is not surprising to see the degree to which Jews copied the practices of all other societies within which they lived. What is surprising is not the degree of similarity but the degree of difference, the level of transcendence, the challenge to oppressive norms. And it was this—the ways the Jews differed from other people precisely because they followed norms that seemed subversive to the established order, and the ways the Jews seemed unwilling to accept "reality" and subordinate themselves to imperial powers—that made them a threat to the ruling elites. Jews were smart enough to know that subversive ideas could create unrest and potentially provoke revolution.

No wonder, then, that ruling elites have had something to gain to the extent that they could turn their own subject populations against the Jews, make them distrust Jews *before* they got too friendly with them and heard the content of what the Jews had to say about how the world did and could work. If subjugated peoples hated the Jews before they had any contact with them, they would be unlikely to listen closely to the story of the Jewish experience with liberation struggles or to attempt to apply that story to their own situation.

I am not suggesting that Jews were a self-conscious revolutionary vanguard plotting to overthrow empires, an ancient-world version of Che Guevara, Trotsky, or Mao Tse-tung. For the most part, Jews did not *consciously* say to themselves that their very existence as Jews was aimed at threatening existing systems of domination around the world (although the Prophetic language of the Jewish people having the task of becoming "a light unto the nations" certainly contained this notion of a world-transforming vanguard). Nor did ruling elites explicitly or consciously articulate their opposition to the Jews in terms of the Jewish role as agents of a revolutionary consciousness. Nevertheless, as the Book of Esther makes clear, even in the ancient world Jews understood that their refusal to act in a subordinate way infuriated ruling elements and provoked anti-Semitic attacks. Nor were Jews always ready to take steps to lessen the conflict. The Aleinu prayer, said three times a day by religious Jews, embodies some of this confrontational spirit. Written at a time when the Persian king called himself "the king of kings," the Aleinu refers explicitly to the Jewish God as the king of the king of kings, and says that Jews will bend their knees to this king alone.

This confrontational spirit and refusal to play along as an obedient client state eventually led the Romans to crush Judea and expel many of its residents, taking tens of thousands as slaves to Rome. To be sure, anti-Semitic feelings were not uncommon among Roman intellectuals, who felt challenged and threatened by the growing numbers of Romans who were turning toward Judaism as a source of ethical and religious inspiration. Seneca denounced Jews for spending "every seventh day without doing anything and thus losing one-seventh part of life," something that he saw as "contrary to a useful life." Tacitus, who bemoaned "Jewish solidarity," the Jews' refusal to have intercourse with non-Jewish women, their refusal to kill "a single child," and their intolerance of any idol or statue, concluded in language that neatly expressed the eternal tension between Roman imperialism and Judaism: "All that we hold sacred is profane to them; all that is licit to them is impure to us." Roman intellectuals intuitively understood the force of the cultural challenge embodied in Judaism. But the Roman ruling elite was more attuned to the political challenge: Jews' continuing refusal to accept the divinity of the caesar manifested a deeper refusal to accept domination within the imperial system. This political challenge needed to be wiped out by the brutal suppression of any form of Jewish independence and the expulsion of Jews from the Roman Empire.

Christian Oppression of Jews

The Romans destroyed the Temple in Jerusalem in 70 C.E., and then forcibly expelled the Jews from the land the Romans had renamed Palestine to show their power to define the language of the realm. Many Christians interpreted these events as a sign that God had rejected the Jews. Judaism competed with Christianity for converts until at least the fifth century, and the argument often proceeded by denigrating the other religion. In the first few centuries after Jesus' death, many Christians had great difficulty explaining why the very people who had known this Jewish man from Samaria had been unimpressed by him, or at least had failed to see him as either "messiah" or "son of God." The elaborate stories of miracles and resurrection made a much bigger impression on the gentiles than on most Jews. One way Christians could account for this was to say the Jews had at one point been chosen, but had lost that status and become outcasts because they had rejected Jesus. The Jews deserved punishment and denigration, these Christians began to argue, because they had rejected the messiah.

In the early years of Christianity, such a doctrine had only a limited effect. The Christians were themselves being persecuted, after all, so it did not work well to emphasize that one could read the objective worth of one's religion by how well it was received by the ruling elite. But once the church assumed state power in the fourth century, Christian triumphalism led to an intensification of persecution of the Jews. Jewish proselytism was outlawed in 329. As Edward Flannery describes it in his classic work, *The Anguish of the Jews: Twenty-three Centuries of Antisemitism,* at the close of the third century (before the triumph of Christianity in the Roman world), the Jew "was no more than a special type of unbeliever; at the end of the fourth, [the Jew was] a semi-satanic figure, cursed by God, and marked off by the State."

A full-scale attack on Jews as "inveterate murderers, destroyers," and "lustful, rapacious, greedy, perfidious bandits" whose synagogues were "the house of the devil" and filled with prostitution (the words of St. John Chrysostom, ca. 344–407) helped generate a popular culture of hatred toward Jews that would grow and be sustained by Church teachings for the next fifteen hundred years.

Legal restrictions soon followed. Anti-Jewish legislation adopted by the Church became the law of the land throughout most of what in

the next centuries became "Christian Europe": Jewish-Christian mar-
riages were forbidden, except in the case of conversion by the Jewish
party; Christians were forbidden to celebrate the Passover with Jews;
Jewish property rights were narrowed; Jews were barred from public
functions and from practicing law; Jews were prevented from testify-
ing against a Christian; the Mishna, and later the Talmud, were
banned; in some countries Jews were forcibly baptized and their
property forcibly expropriated. Eventually, some countries forcibly
expelled their Jews.

There were moments in some Christian countries when church
figures took a different stance, mitigating Jewish persecution for the
sake of keeping the Jewish people alive as living proof of the
degraded state of those who rejected Jesus. There were even some
moments in which relatively humane Christians tried to ease the burden on the Jews.

The Jews were rarely in positions of total powerlessness; often
they had their own communal self-governance or mechanisms of psychological defense (like denigrating non-Jews and seeing themselves
as morally and spiritually superior to their Christian oppressors). Yet
the picture of oppression in the West is well-known, and if it culminated in moments of outright mass murder only periodically, it was
nevertheless the case that most Jews lived under conditions of relative
insecurity generated by a hostile culture, a Christian ruling elite that
manifested contempt and hostility, and a surrounding population that
might at any moment explode in irrational violence against them.

When Christianity first emerged, it shared with Judaism a spirit
of negation of the existing social order. While Judaism tended to suggest that a very different kind of social order could be built in this
world, Christianity seemed to despair of a this-worldly transformation and suggested instead that there was a future world in which the
believer would be rewarded. To the extent that Roman power seemed
invincible and Roman evil pervasive, those who recoiled at Roman
rule were attracted to Christianity because it seemed at once to
embody a rejection of Roman evil while being "realistic" (in the sense
of avoiding the notion that evil could be vanquished in *this* world and
hence relieving followers of the necessity to devote their religious
energies to a struggle with the powers that be)—while still offering a
consolation in the form of belief in other-worldly reward.

But once Christianity took power, it began to weaken its denun-
ciations of this world. As a Christian Europe emerged, the Church

increasingly identified with the powers of this world, saw the established feudal order as sanctified by God, and celebrated the existing
division of wealth and power. Yet the daily life-experience of feudalism for the majority of its participants was often deeply painful and
oppressive. The social solidarity that might have been the expected
result of living in a church-sanctified order was often precarious, and
there was a persistent threat that people would seek some explanation
for why their lives felt so painful.

Throughout human history, when ruling groups have been forced to deal with the inability of their social order to provide deep satisfaction to those whom they have subordinated, one technique that they have frequently resorted to is to find "the Other," some group that is not like the majority, and to blame the problem on that Other. For most of European history, the group that has most consistently been chosen to be this Other has been the Jews.

Not every outburst of anti-Semitism was the direct result of some move by the church or calculation of local leaders to divert angry sentiments onto some potential scapegoat. Once anti-Semitism had been deeply ingrained in the culture of European life, it took on a life of its own, and was passed on from parents to children in every generation. Just as cynicism about the possibility of social change and belief in human selfishness are the "common sense" of contemporary capitalist societies, so anti-Semitism was an intrinsic part of the "common sense" of most European societies once they had been Christianized. That "common sense" continued long after anyone could remember its foundations or why anyone was supposed to believe it. Stories of Jews killing Christian children and using their blood to make matzoh, Jews poisoning wells, or Jews engaging in rapacious sexual behavior were all part of the attempts of the Christian laity to explain to themselves why they were justified in holding these culturally sanctioned and inherited anti-Semitic angers.

Oppression forced Jews to band together tightly, to define rigid boundaries around their communities and lifestyles, and to develop compensatory fantasies about their specialness and the evil of the Christian world. Yet clannishness and separateness were not the preferred responses of Jews to Christian oppression; rather, they were forced upon Jews by legal arrangements that prescribed where Jews could live and travel and what Jews could do to make a living. (The moment the legal restrictions on Jews were removed after the French revolution, Jews poured into the mainstream of European life, attempting to leave behind all separateness and clannish behavior.) While Jews erected powerful psychological defenses to protect themselves, the economic and political degradation of their daily lives, coupled with the constant feeling of being rejected and treated as pariahs, necessarily generated a deep level of isolation, pain, and humiliation that scarred the Jewish psyche. The fierce barriers Jews erected to prevent social contact with non-Jews, the fantasies of revenge on those who had spilled Jewish blood, and the cultural denigration of the intelligence and moral sensibility of non-Jews were the flip side of this pain and the desire for recognition and acceptance.

The Islamic World

Anti-Semitism rarely reached the same fever pitch in Islamic lands as in Christian Europe. While the Koran explicitly denounced Jews, particularly for refusing to accept Muhammad, Arab civilization tended to be more tolerant of and less threatened by the very existence of the Jewish people. Nevertheless, it would be a mistake to use the high level of oppression in the Christian West as the standard by which to judge Islamic treatment of the Jews. Jews were always second-class citizens in Islamic lands—their culture systematically devalued, their property subjected to excessive taxation, and their fates dependent on the good will of whoever was in power.

By standards of the contemporary West, most Jews in Islamic lands lived under conditions at least as harsh as those facing urban blacks under apartheid in South Africa. While some Jews were able to rise to positions of power and influence within the courts of some Islamic potentates, most experienced their treatment as oppressive and precarious, and the collective memory of that oppression persists today in the consciousness of the majority of Oriental Jews (Mizrachim or Sephardim), who constitute the largest ethnic group in Israel today. One reason Jews from Islamic lands have voted for right-wing Israeli parties is that the Right has acknowledged this oppression while the Left has appeared to deny it or belittle it by comparison to the mass murder of European Jews.

Jews and Capitalism

The dispersion of Jews throughout the Christian and Islamic worlds gave Jews a particular advantage in one area—trade. Jews could travel from country to country and find communities that shared basic traditions, language, and a sense of camaraderie in the face of external danger. Nevertheless, the concentration of Jews in

Hepp ! Hepp !

A scene from the "Hep! Hep!" anti-Jewish riots of 1819. The riots, during which German economic woes were blamed on Jewish entrepeneurs and moneylenders, were a factor in accelerating assimilation and confusion among some Jews.

trade was more a function of their exclusion from the major form of wealth and power in the feudal world; namely, the ownership of land. Guilds that emerged in the eleventh to fourteenth centuries almost always excluded Jews, denying them the newly-emerging forms of skilled labor jobs. Similarly, it was the exclusion of Jews from most other ways of making a living that led some Jews into areas like moneylending. These occupations were risky, not only because the ventures could fail, but also because profiting from these activities was deemed unacceptable in the feudal world. Jewish success in these areas became another "reason" for non-Jews to justify hating Jews. If Jews were willing to enter risky occupations, it was only because safer and more contained ways of making a living were systematically closed to them.

Given the disadvantages Jews faced under feudal regimes, it is not surprising that some of them championed the rise of the bourgeoisie. But the rise of the bourgeois order also put many Jews in the middle of an increasingly intense struggle between landlords and peasants, creating an economic niche for Jews that was at once economically rewarding and politically dangerous. As land became "capital" that could be sold by absentee landlords, enclosures of traditionally communal lands put increasing economic pressures on the peasantry. Landowning elites, particularly in Central and Eastern Europe, offered Jews a precarious deal: Jews would provide services to the king, noble, or landowner, in exchange for the "right" to remain on the land, not to pay confiscatory taxes, or to be defended against riotous mobs. Sometimes these arrangements were little more than explicit blackmail or Mafia-style "protection" agreements. But in many places, particularly in Eastern Europe, they became the normal order of the day: Jews as the *public face of the oppressor,* serving as the mediator between the rulers and the subject population. Jews were recruited to become the tax collectors, foremen, innkeepers and liquor distributors for the large landowners and feudal elite. To the ordinary serf or peasant, these Jews seemed to have immense power. It was to them that one had to pay the taxes or levies, to them that one paid for the goods that were being brought in from other areas, and to them that one had to appeal when facing arbitrary decisions of the landowners.

For the Jews, these kinds of economic arrangements were all that was available. The serfs and the peasantry, themselves inheritors of a long history of anti-Semitism, had no inclination to ally themselves with the Jews in any struggle against those with power. On the contrary, they often suspected that it was really the Jews who had the power, and that their Christian overlords were themselves being manipulated by the Jews. So Jews could not become peasants or hope to find support among them. On the other hand, the feudal lords, kings, and others with power carefully circumscribed what occupations Jews could enter, leaving only those that were most risky or most likely to provoke the peasant population.

In good times, these arrangements worked to the temporary benefit of the Jews. Jews had defensively adopted an attitude of contempt for the Jew-hating peasantry, and many Jews had little trouble justifying to themselves the role of representing the landlords' interests. The economic security offered by this arrangement was far preferable to the extreme economic deprivation and hardship that still characterized the lives of the majority of Jewish people in Eastern Europe, who often remained at the economic margins. Many Jews embraced and sought the role of "middleman," but accepting this "deal" had severe costs. Whenever economic contraction led to a restiveness among the peasantry, the ruling elites could manipulate the anger that might otherwise have been directed against themselves and direct it toward the Jews. And since Jews *appeared* to have more power than the rest of the population, it was not hard to stir people up against them. Periodic outbreaks of violence against the Jews served as a convenient alternative to the possibility of violence directed toward the ruling elites.

It was no wonder, then, that Jews hoped for an emancipation from the world in which the Church and its values had shaped popular consciousness against Jews. Nor is it any wonder that the Jews would have welcomed the ideology of capitalism, an ideology that promised them some measure of freedom. If the capitalists could break down the long history of legal oppression of Jews, if they could create a world based on the notion that, regardless of one's social standing, one had an equal right to succeed, they would finally make it possible for Jews to stand on their own feet without the disadvantages imposed upon them by a Jew-hating society. So it's no surprise that between the fifteenth and eighteenth centuries there were Jews who championed the rise of the bourgeoisie.

Those who feared the newly emerging order often directed their anger at the Jews. Traditional societies were repressive in many respects, but the capitalist order that replaced them seemed problematic in new and unexpected ways. The sense of order, regularity, and predictability that made life feel relatively safe was suddenly in danger. Even those who economically or politically benefited from the new capitalist order had some ambivalence about its destabilizing characteristics, and could sympathize with advocates of the old order who lamented the emotional chaos that accompanied the smashing of old orthodoxies. There were many who responded to this new situation by trying to hold on to the past, and who felt angered and upset by all the forces that seemed to be tearing up the old order.

Yet the Jews were the quintessential boundary-smashers. They were a people without a land, unlike other visiting or subject populations—more like gypsies than like anyone else. They identified themselves with breaking down the old order, and benefited in some

Natan Hirschl der Pragerische Judenschafft Pri-
mas, und deß hebräischen Gesatzes approbierter

*"A paragon for all thieves, a rogue, a gallows bird seeking his greatest
happiness in fraud and cunning"; a seventeenth-century German engraving
depicting a Jewish community leader.*

obvious economic and political ways from the destruction of the very traditions that provided comfort to everyone else.

Not that all Jews welcomed the emergence of liberal values and a new social order. While most celebrated the toppling of legal restrictions against Jews in Western Europe in the wake of the revolutions of 1789, 1830, 1848, and 1870, many religious Jews feared the wholesale abandonment of the Jewish people to assimilation. In Eastern Europe, legal emancipation had not yet been fully achieved, and various forms of self-governance had allowed Jewish communities some degree of authority and dignity despite the hostility of the larger society; and so the leaders of the Jewish community in nineteenth-century Eastern Europe saw capitalist triumph as a very mixed blessing. A sizable group of Jews in Eastern Europe made the transition out of the ghettos and pales of settlement not as advocates of the new capitalist order, but as champions of a Jewish socialist vision that sought to build a new world view free of the oppression and exploitation that appeared to be as endemic in capitalism as it had been in feudalism.

The Failures of Emancipation: Anti-Semitism Retains Its Hold

One of the greatest traumas experienced by the Jewish people in the past two hundred years has been the recognition that the decline of Christianity as the dominant force shaping the economic and political realm, the emancipation of Jews from legal restrictions, and the extension of "equal rights as citizens" to Jews did not eliminate anti-Semitism. The impact of centuries of church-sponsored indoctrination against the Jews led to a popular anti-Semitism that continued to flourish throughout most of the nineteenth and twentieth centuries. Nor was there ever any serious effort on the part of the church or the state to educate people about the distortions and dangers of anti-Semitism. Even when, in post-Holocaust revulsion at what Christian Europe had done to the Jews, the Catholic church eliminated its most vicious anti-Semitic teachings and prayers, it did not engage in any sustained or systematic education of its laity about how anti-Semitism had been engendered by the church. Facing no serious attempt to explain why anti-Semitic attitudes were wrong and how people had been indoctrinated to believe them, most Europeans continued to imbibe anti-Semitic attitudes as part of their general culture. While there were some individual Christian leaders who acted to establish communication or support tolerance, there was little systematic effort to integrate into the weekly instruction of the laity any deep understanding of the role Christianity and Christians had played in oppressing Jews and generating a culture of Jew-hating.

Moreover, ruling elites continued to find it useful to exploit anti-Semitic fantasies and to use the Jews as the public face of ruling-class oppression. Jews who had been let into the society rarely found themselves let into the commanding posts in the corporate world. Instead, they were allowed into the middle positions, in which they seemed to enjoy more wealth and power than the average worker or peasant but, in fact, had little more than the power to serve those elites who actually owned land and the means to produce. Many Jews enthusiastically embraced the offer of middle positions, and some even managed to claw their way up the economic ladder to commanding positions in the economy. But by and large, the Jews remained in the same ambiguous position of appearing to have power without really having it.

As the first euphoria about emancipation subsided among Western European Jews, it became increasingly apparent that the revolutionary upsurge of the nineteenth century had failed to eliminate the deeply entrenched anti-Semitism of European societies. Explicitly anti-Semitic parties began to emerge in Western European societies that otherwise seemed to proclaim themselves committed to values of rationalism, science, humanism, and enlightenment. The Dreyfus case in France in the 1890s, in which a Jewish army officer was falsely charged with treason, loosed a torrent of anti-Semitic outbursts that symbolized to many enlightened Jews that they had been too optimistic in hoping that capitalism and legal equality had brought an end to anti-Semitism.

Jewish Reactions to the Persistence of Jew-Hating in the Twentieth Century

Despair about the ability of non-Jews ever to overcome their antagonism toward Jews led many to think that anti-Semitism was proving itself to be an ontological fact of reality, something that would have to be dealt with, but that could never be overcome as long as the Jews kept their identity as a people. Jews responded to persistent anti-

Semitism in the following ways:

1. **Religious Jews** tended to see contemporary anti-Semitism as further proof of the degraded status of the non-Jew and of the need to avoid non-Jewish culture and thought-patterns. Because anti-Semitism was built into the structure of reality, Jews could do little to overcome their suffering until the Messiah was sent by God.

This pessimism, quietism, and despair was a far cry from the revolutionary message of Exodus, the challenging words of the Prophets, or the spirit that led Jews to rebel time after time against Rome. After centuries of oppression, religious Judaism no longer embodied the contentiousness of a people that had seen empires collapse. The remnants of this Jewish religious spark were now concentrated in a ferocious holding-on to the ways things had been done in the past, even at the cost of institutionalizing rigidity and freezing out some of the spontaneity, joy, creativity, and optimism that had sustained the Jewish spirit. The more fearful the religious leaders became, the more they resorted to repression—disciplining those who read the texts of the Emancipation, insisting on stricter and more narrow interpretations of the law, focusing more on the letter than the spirit, and generally acting in narrow-minded and oppressive ways that actually helped accelerate the process of abandoning Judaism. Ironically, the cumulative impact of centuries of oppression had caused religious Judaism to lose some of its most attractive elements—the sighs of pain had begun to drown out the shouts of joy. This is part of the reason why so many Jews sought to leave the religious world as soon as they were given the option.

2. **Assimilationists** thought that the best protection against anti-Semitism would be to use the opportunities Jews had to abandon their distinctive identity. If Jews could merge into the general population and no longer be noticed as a special group, they reasoned, there would be no way for people to hold on to anger at them. While the most extreme assimilationists actually converted, many others attempted to remain Jewish while trying to show the non-Jews that they were "just like them." For some, this involved changing Jewish religious services to make them appear more Christian (organs, flowing robes for rabbis, conducting the service in the language of the country rather than in Hebrew, using ushers and decorum in the sanctuary—even in some cases holding Sabbath ser-

vices on Sunday morning rather than on Saturday). Others changed their names to make them sound more American, or French, or German or English (depending on where they lived). All adopted Western dress and appearance, and by the second half of the twentieth century, some were having operations on their noses or breasts to make them conform more to non-Jewish standards of beauty. Many patterned their speech, their behavior in public places, and their family lives on what they imagined to be the "acceptable behavior" of non-Jews in the society.

Unfortunately, assimilationist strategies seemed to have little impact on non-Jews. The German-Jewish community appeared to be the most highly assimilated in the world, yet the Nazis made a conscious effort to find "Jewish blood" that went back several generations; no matter how polite or goyish the individual Jew acted in her or his life, the Jews still ended up in concentration camps.

3. **Internationalists** thought that the best way to overcome anti-Semitism was for the Jews to reject their national or particularistic identity. Jews should count on solidarity from the international working class, they reasoned, who would soon recognize that their real interests were to oppose every form of national chauvinism and to reject every form of racism. Unfortunately, as we shall discuss briefly in the next chapter, most of the Jews who chose internationalism perished—not only at the hands of the Nazis, but also at the hands of the European proletariat whose anti-Semitism led many to refuse help to the Jews, and led others to join the massacre.

4. **Zionists** believed the only solution for the Jews was to recognize that in a historical period when most people were responding to nationalism, the Jews would need to have their own Jewish state for self-defense. In the next chapters we will consider both the internationalist and Zionist responses and how they fared for the Jewish people.

5. **Allies with the ruling class** assumed anti-Semitism was endemic to the masses, who were fundamentally irrational but could be assuaged if Jews proved that they were faithful servants to the ruling class. The ruling class would, in turn, protect Jewish interests against outbreaks of anti-Semitism. Jews who pursued this line desperately wanted to show that the Jewish people posed no threat to the

ruling interests of the society, could be counted on as good citizens, and would always put the interests of the establishment above "sectarian" Jewish interests. Some who pursued this strategy also adapted a form of assimilation, while others, particularly in the post-1967 period in the U.S., proudly proclaimed their Jewishness in their private life, sometimes even as practitioners of Orthodox Judaism.

This strategy has its problems, since ruling classes have rarely felt that Jews were important enough allies to make serious concessions on their behalf. Instead, they often used Jews in the ways described above—as spokespeople who could be the public face of ruling class interests—and then abandoned them the moment it became convenient to use anti-Semitism to counter rising economic or social discontent. In Europe, for example, Jews were often highly placed in various political regimes where the ruling class would listen to them, but rarely if ever were they willing to defend the Jews when Jews were threatened. In the U.S., the American ruling class showed little interest in using its military power to bomb the railroads leading to the Nazi concentration camps or to open the immigration gates and allow Jews to escape from Nazi Europe. The strategy of alignment with the ruling class, then, seems based on a fundamental misreading of how the ruling class behaves.

One of the most destructive consequences of the "ally of the ruling class" strategy is that it generates popular anger at the Jews. Jews appear not only to be benefiting from ties to the ruling class, but in the eyes of the ill-informed, they appear to *be* the ruling class. Popular discontent then can be swung against the Jews. Thus, anti-Semitism becomes the socialism of fools.

There's another destructive consequence of this strategy: In order to "behave" as a loyal ally, the Jewish community has to abandon much of the Jewish tradition or, more exactly, it has to redefine tradition in ways that will make it consistent with a system of class oppression. The prophetic tradition in Judaism need not be discarded. But it must now be taken as a sweet hope for some other period rather than as a directive for how the Jewish community should organize itself. The rebellious spirit of Judaism and its revolutionary message must be ignored, or the Jewish people must be so deadened to its meaning that they can say the words without even beginning to listen to what they are saying. Part of this transformation has seen the fundraisers and the wealthy become the heroes and rulers of the Jewish world—while the scholars and social activists are ignored, their controversial interpretations treated as an embarrassment or a betrayal, their questions suppressed, their search for spiritual and ethical truths demeaned, ridiculed, or marginalized. Thus, to the extent that the Jewish community makes itself the ally of the ruling class, it simultaneously empties Judaism of its content, and turns this revolutionary religion into a series of rituals and mythic stories that have little to say to contemporary reality. Survival at this price is a subtle form of destruction of the Jewish people.

The common thread between these responses was the knowledge that post-Christian Europeans were likely to reject, disparage, and perhaps fully ignore the humanity of those Jews who intended to remain proud and publicly identify with their religious and national heritage. Subsequent experience in the first half of the twentieth century in a Europe that responded so enthusiastically to anti-Semitism showed that Jewish fears on this score were well-founded.

3

The False Promise of the Left

Ever since Jews were legally emancipated from the ghettos of Europe and given equal rights with their Christian neighbors some 150 years ago, a higher percentage of Jews in Western Europe and the U.S. have been attracted to the organized Left than the percentage of any other ethnic, religious, or national group. Some people have argued that this was only natural—because Jews were the most oppressed group in Western society, and hence the group most likely to pin its hopes on those who were committed to making fundamental changes in the society.

But that can't be the whole story—because other oppressed groups have *not* always been attracted to the Left, even though one might give a similar account of their "objective oppression." Rather, one important element in Jewish openness to the Left was that Jews held an ideological commitment, based in their religion, to see the world as changeable and to see themselves as having an obligation to participate in that transformation. While many Jews who joined the Left were inveterate secularists, their proclivity toward seeing themselves as having an obligation to change the world was, in part, a product of having been raised within a strong Jewish culture, sharing the values, humor, and stories with which their parents and grandparents had grown up. Those parents and grandparents might long ago have abandoned any narrowly defined religious ideas (like an official "belief in God"), but it was much harder to throw off the unconscious hold of the deep Jewish religious commitment to care about the oppressed—rooted in specific injunctions in Torah, and absorbed into the pores of traditional Jewish religious life.

There were, of course, more pressing and immediate reasons for Jews to join the Left. The Left was the only organized political force that specifically acknowledged the racism and oppression facing the Jews and integrated that knowledge into its official list of grievances and concerns. Moreover, the Left proposed a vision of a world in which the oppression Jews faced as Jews, and also the oppression Jews faced as human beings (most particularly, as members of an oppressed working class), would be eliminated.

The Attempt to Assimilate into the Left

Many Jews who entered the Left in the nineteenth and twentieth centuries were *also* assimilationist in their instincts—believing they would be better off and less likely to be persecuted *as Jews* if they could show their non-Jewish neighbors that they were really just like them, that they really could behave in ways that were "inoffensive" (not different from the behavioral patterns of their non-Jewish neighbors), and that they really would not insist on specifically *Jewish* concerns within the Left. It was this last point that led many assimilationist Jews into a very specific kind of internationalism that denied the importance or validity of their own cultural, religious, or national heritage.

Many Jews who were attracted to the Left felt that they needed to show how far they had come from what they perceived to be the repressive and reactionary attitudes of the organized (usually Orthodox-dominated) Jewish community. Rarely able to understand that the Judaism they were seeking to escape was itself a distorted product of centuries of oppression, many of these Jews assumed that Jewish life could mean nothing more than a veil of tears and restrictions. To these Jews, there was no sacrifice in abandoning Judaism in order to fit into the larger Christian society.

Seeing things in this way was itself a product of the previous success of anti-Semitism. When Judaism was allowed to flourish in Spain in the thirteenth and fourteenth centuries, few Jews imagined escaping its reach. It was only when the Inquisition triumphed, and Jews were forced to convert or flee, that the freedom of Jewish life in Spain, with its traditions of joyful living, erotic poetry, and open exchange with non-Jews, gave way to a much more terrified and restrictive Judaism. The expulsion from Spain in 1492 and the subsequent rise of capitalism corresponded with the decline of Jewish fates and the closing of the Jewish religious mind.

The rise of imperialistic nationalism in subsequent centuries placed the Jews in an increasingly precarious situation. As traditional peasant societies were disrupted by the emergence of a national and then an international market, angers that might have been directed at the newly emerging ruling classes were directed at Jews. Instead of the predictable but usually contained hostility that characterized much of the Middle Ages, the early modern period ushered in an intensified level of Jewish oppression. Starting with the expulsion of Jews from Spain in 1492 and intensifying with the Chmelnitzsky massacres of several hundred thousand Jews in Poland in 1648, Jewish life became increasingly dominated by pain, fear, and danger. The result could be read in Judaism and Jewish communal life: a decrease in the self-confidence needed to develop and adapt Judaism and Jewish life to the evolving world, freezing religious forms, repressing dissent, fearing change. These developments were expressed in the daily practices of religious Jews—for example, the adoption of the clothes of Polish landlords of the sixteenth century as the "official outfit" for ultra-Orthodox Jews of the nineteenth and twentieth centuries, or the adoption of religious practices from the fifteenth and sixteenth centuries as definitive for later centuries.

Even the Chasidic religious revivalist movement of eighteenth-century Eastern Europe, which initially counterposed itself to the joylessness and rigidity of the organized Jewish community—as well as to the pseudomessianic movements that provided consolation for Jews reeling at the cumulative pain of expulsion from Spain and then mass murder at the hands of Eastern European mobs—all too quickly accommodated itself to the pattern of ossification that dominated the Jewish religious mainstream. Seeking to legitimize itself in the face of fierce attacks by both Jewish traditionalists and some newly emancipated Jews who saw Chasidism as primitive and ignorant, Chasidic leaders moved away from their initial embrace of a religion of joy and populist impulses to the strictest enforcement of Halacha (traditional Jewish religious law).

Few of those who subsequently assimilated into the non-Jewish world understood how badly the Judaism they were abandoning had been deformed by anti-Semitism. Many of these Jews could understand this kind of reasoning when it concerned other areas of their experience. They could accept and forgive racism among working people by seeing it as a product of previous indoctrination and oppression, without feeling that the hope for a future regime based on workers' power was somehow definitively discredited by the degraded state of workers in nineteenth- and early twentieth-century Europe. But few of these Jewish leftists allowed themselves to take a similarly compassionate view of their own people and its deformations.

Nor is it particularly surprising that a large number of "emancipated" Jews found it difficult to apply the same compassionate attitude toward their own people that they could apply to others. It is typical of oppressed people in the modern world that they adopt a form of self-loathing, blame themselves for their oppression, and share with their oppressors a conviction that the oppressed group is somehow "objectively" worse than others.

Of course, the desire to abandon Judaism and to show how un-Jewish and universal Jews could be was not primarily a product of Jewish self-hatred, but a realistic self-preservative response to the reality of anti-Semitism in European society. Jews who desired to play down their Jewishness were not irrational to believe that being Jewish would be an obstacle to success and acceptance.

It may have been surprising to many Jews to find that *their Jewishness was also an obstacle to success and acceptance on the Left.* But there is considerable evidence to show that this was, and continues to be, as true in the social milieu of the Left as in any other sector of society.

In fact, why should one suspect anything different? Certainly it would be no shock to learn that there is sexism and racism among people on the Left in contemporary Western societies. We all understand that those who have been socialized in a racist or sexist society are likely to have imbibed its major prejudices. So why should we be surprised that the same is true of anti-Semitism?

> **It would have been the greatest of miracles, and totally without possible rational explanation, had European societies, drenched in centuries of Jew-hating, produced a Left that was not deeply stained by anti-Semitism.**

Given the inevitable inheritance of Jew-hating on the Left, those Jews who wished to be accepted there were faced with the following options: to insist on the importance of their Jewishness and be marginalized within the mainstream of the Left; to develop a separate Jewish Left; or to downplay their Jewishness and assure their fellow leftists that they were not "too Jewish."

So just as sexism has flourished in leftist parties that officially advocated equality for women, so anti-Semitic attitudes and demands have flourished in parties that officially condemned anti-Semitism. Yet precisely because leftist parties officially condemned anti-Semitism, the contradiction did not appear obvious to the Jewish leftists who tried to penetrate the mainstream, believing that downplaying their Jewishness was a scant price to pay to become part of a socialist movement that articulated internationalist, pacifist, and anti-nationalist ideas.

Holding on to Jewish Identity and Left Identities: The Bund

While the assimilationist road seemed most appealing to many Jews in Western Europe and the U.S. in the early twentieth century, the Jewish working masses of Eastern Europe were not confronted with a society that seemed as open to Jewish assimilation as those in the West. Often living in an all-Jewish world, Eastern European Jewish workers struggled against the Jewish rich. According to Jewish historian Howard Sachar, by the beginning of the twentieth century, 40 percent of the Jewish population of the Pale was proletarianized.

Those who sought to organize these Jewish workers found that they were far more successful using Yiddish rather than Russian as the language of socialist agitation. A Jewish socialist organization, the Bund, led important strikes that won significant improvements in working conditions, while successfully evading the secret police. The Bund tied its opposition to class oppression to an explicit commitment to fight the national oppression of one nationality by another, and it insisted on the importance of "legitimate Jewish national rights." Much like those who in the latter half of the twentieth century sought independence and autonomy for African Americans, women's, and gay and lesbian voices within the Left, the Bund demanded cultural autonomy for Jews both within the Left and the larger society that the Left was striving to create.

The largest challenge to the Bund came from the Zionist movement, which urged young Jews to leave the Galut (exile outside of Palestine) and join in building a Jewish state—a position that Bundists denounced as "bourgeois utopianism." Though Zionism grew increasingly popular with middle- and lower-middle-class Jews, the Bund became the primary political force in the Jewish working class between 1900 and 1914, playing a central role in the revolution of 1905 and in the continuing struggle against the Czar.

The Bund's particular strength was its unique integration of politics and culture. As Sachar puts it, "socialism was conceived by the Bundists not merely as a new system of social economy, but as a new civilization, as an entirely new way of life." Poetry, fiction, and philosophy—all in Yiddish—were a central part of the political struggle.

The Bund won enthusiastic support from Jewish workers, as well as from many of those middle-class intellectuals who were not drawn to Zionism. Moreover, it was a major force in pre-Bolshevik Russia. As historian Nora Levin wrote, in her book *The Jews in the Soviet Union Since 1917,* "The Bund could justifiably claim to have more worker cohesiveness, unity and class support than any other social democratic organization in Russia up to the Bolshevik Revolution."

Although a major force within the Left, the Bund was not the dominant force within the Jewish community, which still had large numbers of people tied to an antimodernist, religious traditionalism or to various forms of Zionism. Socialist Zionists, attempting to synthesize Marxism and Zionism, followed Ber Borokhov's notion that the only way to correct the economic and social distortions of Jewish life in the Diaspora was for Jews to go to Palestine, set up a Jewish society, and engage in a class struggle within the context of a Jewish society.

Jews were not becoming proletarianized in Russia, argued the socialist Zionists; rather, they were becoming *luftmenschen,* a rootless mass of petty traders and laborers in declining parts of the economy. These Jews would not be integrated, but rather choked into extinction, argued the Borokhovists—and the only future was to leave the abnormal conditions of Diaspora life and set up a society where Jews would not be prevented from developing like any other nation in the world.

Bundists, in turn, attacked the "counterrevolutionary" nature of Zionism, seeing it as draining energy and resources from the real struggle facing Jews in Eastern Europe.

Struggle Between the Bund and the Communists

The Bund's insistence on cultural and political autonomy made it suspect to the Bolsheviks, particularly after the Bund had embraced the Kerensky government and rallied to its promise of autonomy for all non-Russian people. Imagine how different history might have been if the Bundist struggle for democracy, national and cultural autonomy—and hence a Russia led by a federalized party— had triumphed!

Lenin and Stalin may have disagreed on how a Soviet society should look, but they shared an underlying hostility to any form of nationalism. In his essay "Marxism and the National and Colonial Question," published in 1913, Stalin defined the nation as "a historically evolved stable community of language, territory, economic life, and psychological make-up manifested in a community of culture." As Nora Levin noted, since the Jews had no territory, they were by definition excluded as a legitimate nation. Rejecting the more expansive definitions of a nation as "a cultural community no longer tied to the soil" or "an aggregate of people bound into a community of character by a community of fate" (definitions other socialists put forward to legitimatize a Jewish national identity), Stalin explicitly attacked those who thought that Jewish fate or "certain relics of national character" could possibly form a basis for a future Jewish people. Like Lenin, Stalin rejected the Bundist program of extra-territorial autonomy as "a refined species of nationalism" that would claim autonomy for "a nation whose future is denied and whose present existence remains to be proved."

As early as 1903, Lenin called the Bundist idea of Jewish national autonomy a "Zionist idea ... false and reactionary in its essence. The idea of a separate Jewish people, which is utterly untenable scientifically, is reactionary in its political implications.... Everywhere in Europe the downfall of medievalism and the development of political freedom went hand in hand with the political emancipation of the Jews ... and their ... progressive assimilation by the surrounding population.... [T]he idea of a Jewish nationality is manifestly reactionary.... [It] is in conflict with the interests of the Jewish proletariat for, directly or indirectly, it engenders in its ranks a mood hostile to assimilation, a 'ghetto' mood" (cited in Levin, p. 17).

Lenin counterposed bourgeois national culture to proletarian internationalist culture. Although the elements of a democratic, socialist culture are present in every national culture, he wrote, every nation possesses a dominant culture, the culture of the landlords, the clergy, and the bourgeoisie. And "Jewish culture," Lenin wrote in his essay, *Critical Remarks on the National Question,* "is the slogan of rabbis and bourgeoisie, the slogan of our enemies.... Whoever, directly or indirectly, puts forward the slogan of Jewish 'national culture' is (whatever his good intentions may be) an enemy of the proletariat, a supporter of all that is outmoded and connected with caste among the Jewish people; he is an accomplice of the rabbis and bourgeoisie.... [The Bundists] are in effect instruments of bourgeois nationalism among the workers."

Responding to these kinds of charges, the Bundist Pesach Liebman argued in 1913 that "international culture is not non-national.... [Non-national culture], which must not be Russian, Jewish, or Polish, but only pure culture, is nonsense. International ideas can appeal to the working class only when they are adapted to the language spoken by the worker, and to the concrete national conditions under which he lives" (cited in Levin, p. 20). The Bundists had their own approach, and they were not prepared to accept a view that counterposed the long historical traditions and developed cultures of existing national communities to a muddle-headed internationalism that had never attracted support beyond a small community of disenfranchised intellectual dreamers. The Bundists fervently adhered to internationalist aspirations, but they refused to see them as contradictory to Jewish national particularism.

Unlike Stalin, Lenin was not personally an anti-Semite, and in 1914 he publicly fought against anti-Semitism and the persecution of the Jews under the Czar. He was unafraid to state that "No nationality in Russia is so oppressed and persecuted as the Jewish.... During the past few years, the persecution of the Jews has assumed incredible dimensions." Moreover, once in power and faced with the need to hold together a country, Lenin accepted the preservation of national languages and cultures "at least until the economic development had eroded the social and psychological need for national loyalties."

The Continuing Attack on the Jews After the Revolution

Although the Civil War forced Lenin to compromise on some fundamental points, the Bolshevik position remained that the Jewish people would disappear once anti-Semitism had disappeared; because anti-Semitism itself was merely the product of capitalist exploitation, and socialism would soon overcome capitalism, anti-Semitism would quickly become a thing of the past. If this would happen by itself, the post-revolution Bolsheviks argued, then cultural autonomy could be allowed in the meantime. But, as Levin notes, this Bolshevik commitment to cultural autonomy, whether in reference to the Jews or to anyone else, often meant little more than "the right to disseminate centrally issued directives in many languages, later euphemistically phrased by Stalin: 'national in form, but socialist in content.'" And regardless of Lenin's understanding of the need to make accommodations with existing national communities, many of his followers in the Party were less sophisticated and set about as quickly as possible to eradicate all forms of bourgeois nationalism— which in practice meant eradicating all forms of cultural autonomy.

It was the Jews in the Party who became a major vehicle for suppressing Jewish national life after the 1917 revolution. The Jewish Sections of the Bolshevik party, the Evsektsiya, could justify its feeling that Jewish autonomy was no longer necessary by pointing to the new possibilities that had been opened to Jews by the revolution. By 1922, Jews were 5 percent of the Communist party and had a visible presence in the ranks of the secret police (the Cheka). Though Jews represented less than 2 percent of the population of the Ukraine, they comprised 19.9 percent of all personnel in the Ministry of Justice. Jews were allowed into the universities; in the Ukraine in 1923, 47.4 percent of all students at institutions of higher learning were Jews, and many Jews were being accepted on the faculties of the universities. But as individual Jews were allowed into the new society being formed by the Bolsheviks, Jewish communal life came under increasing attack. As early as 1918, Evsektsiya proclaimed that "There is no longer any place in our life for the various institutions which have so far been running things in the Jewish street, for Jewish communities elected by universal, direct suffrage and the secret ballot." Decrees were signed banning the teaching of Hebrew, suppressing religious instruction, and abolishing all Jewish organizations.

The logical organization to resist the crude attempts at bolshevization of the Jewish community would have been the Bund. But the Russian Whites, like many Polish nationalists, had begun a systematic campaign of persecution and violence against the Jews during the Civil War with the Bolsheviks, thus pushing Jews to seek the protection of the Red Army. On the other hand, the Civil War had also led many hard-line Communists to feel that they could no longer tolerate a society of competing parties. So there was immense pressure on the Bund to merge with the Communist party, and by 1921 many local Bund groups had effectively dissolved themselves and entered the Party.

Jewish Communists were in the forefront of the attack on traditional Jewish institutions. To prove their allegiance to Communist internationalism, they were particularly harsh on their own people. Levin cites the writing of one Jewish Communist, Esther Frumkin, who stated clearly the emerging perspective of former Bundists who were now actively engaged in the suppression of Jewish religious life: "You do not understand the danger Jews face. If the Russian people begin to feel that we are partial to Jews, it will be harmful to Jews.... The danger is that the masses may think that Judaism is exempt from anti-religious propaganda. Therefore, Jewish Communists must be even more ruthless with rabbis than non-Jewish Communists are with priests."

The Jewish communists agitated against religion in a series of show trials accusing various Jewish institutions of being bourgeois. Levin describes one such public trial in Kiev in which a defendant "admitted" that she sent her children to cheder (Jewish day school) to avoid having them learn Communist ideas. A rabbi told the audience that he poisoned Jewish youth with religious fairy tales and chauvinistic ideas "deliberately to keep the masses of people in ignorance and bondage to the bourgeoisie," and a stout man bedecked with gold and diamonds "admitted" that the Jewish bourgeoisie used religion to keep the Jewish masses in slavery. Those in the audience who loudly objected to the obvious phoniness of the "confessions" were themselves arrested on the spot. Synagogues were forcibly closed under threat that the Evsektsiya would take members of the synagogue committees to the central authorities unless they complied.

Zionist and Hebrew cultural institutions faced even more intense repression. Zionist offices and newspapers were closed and Zionist leaders were arrested. The Jewish Communists in the Evsektsiya depicted "any harrassment of Zionism as the spontaneous and justified expression of progressive Jewish opinion" against Jewish bourgeois nationalism. Throughout the 1920s, thousands of Zionists were arrested. Evektsiya hailed Yiddish as the language of the masses but denounced Hebrew as the language of bourgeois capitalists, Zionists, and rabbis. The Hebrew presses were nationalized in 1919 and put at the disposal of the Evsektsiya to be used to publish materials in Yiddish. Yet the repression only lent further fuel to the Zionist contention that normal life for the Jewish people was impossible in the Diaspora. Zionists noted that Jewish life was being forcibly repressed—and the main agents of that repression were Jews who wanted to show their full commitment to the universalist program.

Evsektsiya's rejection of Jewish particularism had little impact on the anti-Semitism that pervaded the larger Russian society. In fact, many Russians and other nationalist groups felt that the Communist revolution itself was nothing more than Russia falling under the spell of a Jewish conspiracy. After all, not only was there a disproportionate number of Jews in the Party, but there were many prominent Jews among the top leadership. To Russian, Ukrainian, and other nationalists, it made little difference that Jewish Bolsheviks were doing their best to show that they were not "too" Jewish. Anti-Bolshevik feeling among the masses was frequently associated with anti-Semitism; when the various nationalist and religious groupings that were suppressed in the 1920s made their reappearance in Russia in the late 1980s and early 1990s, these Jew-hating tendencies remained intact.

Once the Bolsheviks had firmly established their power, they never made any full-scale assault on anti-Semitism in the Communist world, other than to make it illegal. There was never any attempt to confront the anti-Jewish myths and stereotypes that had been fostered throughout the past centuries and that remained part of the cultural legacy of many Soviets. On the contrary, the Stalinists themselves used these myths when they sought to strike out against Jews who happened to be their political enemies, most notably against the Jewish Communist Leon Trotsky and those who supported him.

Popular resentment of Jews, solidified throughout hundreds of years of Russian Orthodox and Czarist anti-Semitic indoctrination, remained a major feature of Russian life under Communism. The new opportunities used by Jews to find employment in factories or education in universities now became a "reason" for anti-Jewish feeling. Aid from relatives in the United States allowed some Jews to buy food that other Russians did not have—and this too intensified resentment.

As subsequent evidence now shows, the level of anti-Semitism among Stalinist and post-Stalinist henchmen never abated, and Jews were in constant danger of once again becoming the target of these attacks. Jews inside the Communist party were particularly vulnerable during the great purges of the 1930s: Trotsky, Kamenev, Zinoviev, and other explicit targets were Jewish, and many of those who supported Trotsky were Jewish. Hundreds of thousands of Jews were among the estimated seven million people murdered in the frenzy of bloodletting as Stalin urged his people to sweep the country free of its internal enemies.

Jewish Communists were accused of conspiring with the Nazis and plotting to kill Stalin. The notion that the Jews were particularly likely to betray their Russian neighbors and align with an enemy became a part of the covert message of the struggle against Trotskyites and other deviationists. Sadly, but by this point predictably, many of the prosecution witnesses and agents provocateurs used against the leading Kremlin Jews were also of Jewish origins; they too were eventually killed in the ever-widening circle of the purges. Virtually the entire generation of Jewish Communists who had fought for socialist ideals and become enthusiastic supporters of the revolution in its early days—including most of the leaders of Evsektsiya—were wiped out in the purges.

In Western Europe and the U.S., where Communist parties continued to grow and recruit many Jews, the anti-Jewish aspects of the purges were ignored, denied, or rationalized. Jewish Communists continued to insist that the Jewish question could be solved by ending capitalism, and that no special attention need be given to anti-Semitism or to the possibility that anti-Semitism might persist after the socialist revolution, or within the Communist party itself. In the U.S. and elsewhere, many Jews were attracted to the Communist party (CP), not only because of its courageous work on behalf of the poor and the oppressed, but also, and importantly, because it seemed the political force most committed to fighting fascism. In the period when Hitler was gaining popular support in Germany, the CP had diverted much of its energies to fighting the Social Democrats; but once Hitler took power, the CP adopted the "United Front Against Fascism" strategy, in large part because it understood that Hitler would eventually want to crush the Communist experiment in the Soviet Union. While conservatives talked of "America first" and opposed involvement in the struggle to stop Hitler, the Communists

Moishe Lirvakov (1875-1937), editor-in-chief of the main Yiddish Party newspaper Der Emes (Truth) *entered the communist party along with other former members of socialist and Zionist-socialist parties and was active in the campaigns against Hebrew and Judaism. In 1937 he was arrested as an "enemy of the people." He died in prison that year.*

were on the front line of the fight against the Nazis, and were the bulwark of the forces that went to Spain in 1937 as part of the International Brigade assembled to fight Franco's fascist Black Shirts. Particularly in the U.S., Jews were appreciative of the role the Communists were playing in fighting Hitler, and played a prominent role in the leadership of the Communist party and were among its most vociferous defenders.

Imagine their surprise when Stalin signed a pact with Hitler in 1939. Though some Jews defended the move as Stalin's clever attempt to buy time to build his forces for the inevitable battle with the Nazis, most were deeply distressed by the way Communist parties around the world quickly abandoned any focus on the evils of fascism in general, and Nazi anti-Semitism in particular. Inside the Soviet Union, the Third Reich was congratulated for its struggle against the Jewish religion. According to one account, Stalin promised Hitler that he would eliminate Jews from leading positions the moment he could find sufficient qualified gentiles to replace them. In the section of Poland taken over by the Soviets, leading Polish Jewish Communists were denounced as Trotskyists, and many were imprisoned. Antifascism was suddenly removed from the agenda, not only of the Communist party of the Soviet Union, but of Communist parties around the world. Yet there were many Jews on the Left who told one another that it would be sectarian or chauvinistic to complain about a policy that had abandoned the struggle against anti-Semitism.

When Hitler abandoned this pact and invaded the Soviet Union, the Left was quick to reassert its focus on the evils of fascism and anti-Semitism and to support the Allies. Yet Jews reeling from this first betrayal were soon faced with an even more devastating set of stories of betrayal by the Communist parties and leftist forces in Europe. According to Communist theory, the working classes of Europe were supposed to be most likely to resist fascism. Yet the evidence showed something more complex: The working classes were split, and many working-class people were attracted to a right-wing nationalism that either became explicitly fascist or collaborated with fascist forces.

Many Jews had rejected the overtures of Zionism, believing that when push came to shove, the security of the Jewish people would best be defended by the development of class consciousness in Europe. Instead, they found that even their non-Jewish neighbors and friends, friendly enough in the 1920s and early 1930s, were willing to do little to stand up and fight for them, to protect them, or even to hide them.

There are tens of thousands of important stories of "righteous gentiles" who stood in solidarity with the Jewish people. Yet the overall record was deeply disappointing for those who believed in the possibility of overcoming anti-Semitism. At each stage in the progressively worse oppression of Jews—from anti-Jewish legislation to exclusion from employment, to acts of violence against individual Jews on the streets, to systematic campaigns of violence against Jewish businesses, to deportations and systematic extermination of the Jews—non-Jewish onlookers covered their eyes, shut their doors to

Jews being shot and buried alive. Since Communist papers downplayed Nazi attempts to wipe out the Jews of Eastern Europe, many Jews were unprepared for the murderous campaign waged by German troops and Ukranian nationalists.

people seeking refuge, and in too many cases, became active participants in the process of exterminating the Jews, grabbing their property, and exposing their hideouts.

One would have hoped that this would not be the case among

those on the Left who had been part of an internationalist movement and who were committed to fighting the Fascists. Unfortunately, even in the official organizations of the underground and among the partisans fighting in the forests of Eastern Europe, Jews found that they were not only at risk of deportation, but also subject to the anti-Semitism that flourished among the freedom fighters and leftists. Jews in these resistance groups were sometimes forced to return to the Nazi-controlled areas they had fled, and were sometimes shot or betrayed to anti-Semitic nationalist groups that were actively assisting the Nazis in their murder of Jews.

The Communist parties of Europe had done little to develop an understanding of the dangers of anti-Semitism among their own members. They had given no special attention to fighting racist ideas among party members or to equipping them to fight these ideas in the larger working class. Once the war with Hitler broke out, the Communists did not use Hitler's anti-Semitism as a major reason for opposing him. On the contrary, they stayed away from any attempts to identify the war as a struggle against anti-Semitism. Recognizing the deeply rooted anti-Semitism among the peoples over whom they ruled, the Communist parties often thought that it would be more "effective" for them to show that they were *not* motivated in their antifascist struggle by any particular desire to save the Jews.

As a result, Soviet newspapers and their allies in Eastern Europe did not report on the mass slaughter of the Jews by the Nazis. When the Nazis invaded Lithuania, the Ukraine, and White Russia in 1941, few of the Jewish inhabitants there were prepared for the mass executions that followed. The Jewish victims of these executions were described by the Communist press as "Poles," "Lithuanians," "Latvians," or "Ukrainians," and the Nazi mass murder of the Jews was simply not mentioned. It was only in the period following the overthrow of the Communist party in 1991 that Eastern Europeans began to acknowledge that Jews were the victims of the Nazi invasion.

Jews who attempted to organize resistance in Warsaw and other cities in Nazi-occupied Eastern Europe reported that they had great difficulty obtaining material aid and political support from the gentile-led Communist and Socialist organizations that functioned as the civilian underground. Resistance organizations were often filled with anti-Semites, or were fearful that they would not be able to do business with the anti-Semites whose help they needed if they were to become clearly aligned with efforts to provide guns, ammunition, or other forms of assistance to the Jews. While there were many instances in which Communists and Socialists fought valiantly on behalf of Jews and tried to get the various underground anti-Nazi organizations to protect and defend Jews, many Jewish survivors contend that this support was rarely consistent or predictable. In interviews I conducted in Israel and the U.S. with ghetto resistance fighters and survivors of partisan units in the forests of Eastern Europe, the story of betrayal and abandonment by those whom Jewish leftists thought they could trust was a recurrent theme—and the basis for a deep disillusionment and despair about the possibilities of Diaspora life for the Jewish people.

It was this constant sense of being on treacherous and unpredictable ground that led many Jewish leftists to become Zionists after World War II. Jews being killed by their fellow freedom fighters during the Polish reconquest of Warsaw, Jews being murdered by their neighbors when they returned to their home towns from concentration camps, antifascist Jewish leaders being murdered by Stalin's orders, and the continuing refusal on the part of the Left, even after the facts of the Holocaust became known, to acknowledge that there was some special problem facing the Jewish people that could not be reduced to an outgrowth of the class struggle—all this contributed to the Jews' growing feeling that they needed to rethink their attachment to the Left.

Particularly in the West, where anticommunism had replaced antifascism as the unifying theme of political life, it was very easy for many Jews to abandon their previous commitments to communism or other forms of left-wing ideology. First, the Left had abandoned and often betrayed the Jewish people. Second, the major Left force in the 1940s and 1950s, the Communist party, still defended Stalin, denied the purges and anti-Semitism in the Soviet Union, and was simply blind to the evils of attempting to identify lofty socialist ideals with the perverted realities of Soviet totalitarianism. Finally, even leftists who were *not* providing ideological cover for the Communist party were nevertheless still unable to develop categories of thought that would enable them to understand or acknowledge the reality of Jewish experience or the massiveness of Jewish suffering. Faced with the murder of six million Jews, the Left during the post-Holocaust years had little to say. Instead, they focused their attention elsewhere, and avoided coming to grips with the meaning the destruction of European Jewry had for their own theories or understanding of the world.

It is *not* my contention that those Jews who turned away from liberal or progressive politics on these grounds were making the correct move. While I sympathize with their anger at the Left, I do not sympathize with those who went on to embrace the worst aspects of capitalism or who became apologists for the emerging new imperial order under the hegemony of the United States. Those of us on the democratic Left emphatically rejected Soviet totalitarianism and enthusiastically embraced America's democratic and human rights aspirations—without shutting our eyes to the hurtful, oppressive or humanly damaging aspects of the competitive market system and of patriarchal social realities.

I personally believe that the socialist vision is inadequate, because it is based on too narrow an understanding of human needs and does not adequately speak to the deepest spiritual, ethical, and psychological dimensions of human reality. But what is correct about the Left's perspective—its commitment to remaking the social world according to principles of justice and fairness ought not to be discarded just because Left rhetoric has been appropriated by paranoid murderers and thugs claiming to be communists to justify oppressive regimes or just because the Left has been deeply tainted by anti-Semitism. Just as Leftists have been influenced by the sexism and racism and materialistic values of the societies within which they have been socialized, so Leftists reflect and imbibe the deep anti-Semitism of the larger world.

It makes more sense, then, to temper our criticism of the Left with the understanding that every liberatory social movement (including the one that Jews started when we overcame slavery and bound ourselves to the voice we heard at Sinai) reflects the fundamental limitations, distortions, and flaws of the human beings who develop and shape it. The task is to struggle against the distortions while remaining committed to the fundamental liberatory aspirations these movements attempt to actualize in the world. Yet given the ugly history of anti-Semitism in the Left, Jews are right to be suspicious, right to want to protect themselves with a Jewish state, and right to insist that the Left give higher priority to teaching about its own failures on this front in the past and to rooting out overt or covert anti-Semitism in its current practices.

Jews can't give up the Left stance—the commitment to critiquing what is in the name of what ought to be, the commitment to transforming the world to make it in accord with Judaism's vision of justice and love—without giving up Judaism itself. What we can do is insist that the Left change the way it understands and deals with the Jewish people.

4

Zionism: Its Legitimacy and Tragic Flaws

The deep pessimism of many Jews in the face of renewed outbursts of anti-Semitism in supposedly enlightened and emancipated late-nineteenth-century Europe produced a surge of interest in Zionism.

Jews had never voluntarily left the land of Israel and Judea—they had been victims of an imperial system whose various successors still governed much of the world. Indeed, while many Jews had been forced out of Palestine at the hands of Roman imperialists, a significant presence remained there until the Arabs conquered and Islamicized the society. Arab rule forcibly prevented Jews from returning through most of the ensuing centuries, although eventually a small community of religious Jews was allowed to establish itself, first in Tzfat, and later in Jerusalem.

Although Zionism was in part a political reaction to the reappearance of anti-Semitism and the growing climate of nationalism in nineteenth-century Europe, the Zionist ideal of Jews returning to their land was also an inherent part of Jewish religion. In every religious service, Jews prayed for a return to Zion; every time a Jew had a meal, she or he called on God to rebuild Jerusalem and to "lift the bonds of our oppression from our necks and lead us speedily back to our land." While most envisioned this return as something that must be left to God to accomplish, there was a continuous and deep yearning for a return to the homeland that spoke deeply to the soul and emotions of most Jews throughout the nineteen centuries in which they were kept from it.

Acquiring the Land in the Early Twentieth Century

Zionism took this yearning and gave it concrete political expression. The Zionists, overwhelmingly secular and hostile to what they saw as passivity and powerlessness in Jewish life in the Diaspora, believed that Jews would only be able to achieve real dignity and empowerment when they took their messianic yearnings out of the realm of religious mysticism and placed them in the realm of practical politics. While David Biale's *Power and Powerlessness in Jewish History* demonstrates that Zionists exaggerated the degree of Jewish powerlessness throughout the centuries of Diaspora, and similarly exaggerated what kind of real autonomy and self-governance a Jewish state could have in a world governed by economic and political superpowers, for many Jews the Zionist notion of creating a Jewish state in the land of their ancestors provided the first encounter with a healthy self-affirmation that was unavailable either in the self-blaming worldview of the religious ("because of our sins we have been exiled from our land") or in the self-renunciation of Jewish leftists.

The claim that Zionism was essentially an extension of Western colonialism makes little sense once one understands the history of oppression of the Jewish people. The Jews were not an integrated and accepted element in colonial Europe, and most who were attracted to Zionism saw it as a way to protect themselves against the oppression of Europe rather than as a vehicle to extend European power or culture. Moreover, the vast majority of Jews who actually came to settle in Palestine in the early aliyot (waves of immigration) came from Eastern Europe, fleeing oppression and despairing of ever changing the deeply ingrained anti-Semitism of the Christian world. Their motivation was to escape centuries of oppression, not to overpower or exploit some other group.

Nevertheless, it's not hard to see why Arabs regarded the waves of Jewish immigration as a colonial phenomenon. First, some important early Zionist leaders like Theodor Herzl and then Chaim Weizmann, appealed to the major colonial powers to realize that a Jewish state could be in their interests. Of course, this was not restricted to appealing to specifically European interests—Herzl, for example, was equally interested in appealing to the Ottomans. Once the Zionists felt their goal was legitimate, they were not averse to trying to play power politics with whoever had power. They were "realists"—but so were all the other players on the scene. For example, to the extent that the Palestinians were organized politically, they found it convenient to ally themselves with the ruling classes in the Islamic world. These ruling classes were every bit as oppressive as any in Europe, even though their powerlessness relative to Europe made it impossible for them to actualize their own deep religious and cultural commitments to Islamicize the world. Furthermore, many of the advocates of national independence in the Third World tried to show the large imperial powers that their aspirations were not in conflict with, and might even advance, the interests of the colonizing country. So it's usually an indication of double standards when one hears Zionism attacked because some of its initial proponents tried to make deals with colonial interests.

Second, there was the fact that Jews started to arrive in Palestine and to buy up land, often from Arab landlords who were no longer present, and to then throw the native Palestinian population off these lands so they could cultivate them. Not all Jewish settlement activity involved displacement—there were enough instances in which Jews were involved in transforming swamplands into arable land to give some substance to the notion that the Zionists were building up the land from nothing. Yet the Zionist excuse that the settlers were simply "a people without a land for a land without a people" was a willed blindness to the actual systematic dispossession of Palestinians that was an integral part of Jewish settlement.

The resentment that the dispossessed Palestinian peasants felt was similar to the resentments felt by peasants throughout Europe in the seventeenth, eighteenth, and nineteenth centuries, as the enclosure movements pushed millions of people from the lands their families had cultivated for hundreds of years. Yes, somewhere, someone held a piece of paper that gave him, and not those who cultivated the land, legal ownership. But that had never meant anything in the past except the responsibility of the peasant to pay rent. Now, suddenly, someone was coming around and telling these peasants that they had to leave the land, providing no viable means for the peasants to support themselves and no place for them to go. Just as the peasants in Europe had responded with anger and upset, so Palestinians responded by giving support to a nationalist movement that wished to stop the expropriations by dispossessing the dispossesors.

The resistance and reaction were understandable. But were the Jews who came to settle colonialists or racists? To answer that question, you have to be sure that you would answer it the same way anywhere you find people using the workings of the capitalist market in ways that unintentionally disadvantage others. For example, later in the same century we had a major migration of the children of white suburbanites into parts of the city that had been previously occupied by African Americans. Partly by using the "urban renewal" powers of the city, partly by sheer economic muscle, these young middle-class whites managed to buy up inner city real estate and, by raising rents, eventually pushed out hundreds of thousands of urban Blacks. Would we say that these people were colonialists or racists? Certainly the policies they pursued had racist consequences, and to the extent that they raised real estate values and helped rebuild the inner cities, these whites also were serving the interests of large corporations with heavy urban real estate investments whose worth might have otherwise declined.

When people operate legally in accord with the logic of the dominant economic system, one can condemn them to the extent that they don't struggle to change the entire system; but if the system is hard to change, and they meanwhile act as rational agents within it, how culpable are they? Probably somewhat, but how much? Would you support demands that middle-income white city dwellers "give back" the land they bought to those former urban dwellers who had been pushed out? What if the former residents had resorted to armed struggle—would they be justified in individual acts of terrorism against the new residents? More likely you'd agree that the real culprits were *not* the whites returning to the city, but rather the economic system as a whole that created an objective conflict between the two groups. One might say that in this circumstance, the middle-class white returnees had *more* responsibility than the previous inner-city residents, because they had more social power. But to bring the analogy back to the Middle East, one could hardly argue that it is obvious that Jews at the end of the nineteenth and beginning of the twentieth centuries had more social power on the world scene than the Arabs. Most who came to Palestine came to escape conditions of overt physical and legal oppression. It is more reasonable to conclude that this is a situation in which two groups, each with relative power in some respects and relative powerlessness in other respects, were set into opposition for reasons that were largely not the fault of either.

Unlike the European enclosure movement, however, which was fought out as a class struggle, the dispossession of Palestinians was fought out in national terms. It was the Jewish people who were buying the land, and individual Jews who were moving in and starting to build a Jewish settlement on what had previously been Arab land. Yet the actual Jews who moved in were *not,* by and large, those with money or power. The land purchases were typically made through the agency of the Jewish National Fund, which in turn collected money from the Jews of Western Europe and America who were ideologically committed to providing a home for Jewish resettlement. Those who actually came to Palestine tended to be relatively impoverished refugees from European oppression—and these refugees had little understanding of the anger of the Palestinian masses. From the standpoint of these refugees, there was plenty of land in the huge Islamic world, so Palestinian resistance was understood to be primarily a manifestation of Arab racism.

Palestinians Paying the Price for a History of Arab Racism

Arab racism toward Jews did not start with Zionism. Jews had been systematically oppressed for centuries in Islamic lands (for a detailed account, see historian Norman Stillman's book *The Jews of Arab Lands in Modern Times*). Many Oriental Jews had welcomed European colonialism in North Africa and the Middle East, because the Europeans promised to curtail the worst effects of discriminatory legal and social systems that had been an integral part of Jewish life in Arab lands. Arab society had both ideological and legal mechanisms for suppressing Jewish rights. Those Arabs who lived under the British mandate in Palestine rarely identified themselves as Palestinians—they saw themselves as part of the great Arab nation of Islamic people that extended from Iraq to Morocco. But if we understand them as part of the Arab nation, we also must see that they were part of a people that had for a long time benefited from the systematic exploitation and repression of Jews.

This point is important because we can understand Zionism as a program of affirmative action for Jews on a world scale. For nineteen hundred years, most of the peoples of the world had treated the Jews as people to be oppressed, exploited, robbed, raped, and murdered. Now, in the modern era, some Christians began to understand that the Jewish people deserved some compensation for all they had undergone. Particularly after the Holocaust, when one in every three

Jews had been murdered, the world community agreed that the Jews should be granted a state like most other peoples.

Fine, some Palestinians answer, but why should that affirmative action take place at *our* expense. After all, it was not *we* who caused the Holocaust. True enough. But neither were the Palestinian people totally innocent bystanders, with no relationship to Jewish oppression. Part of the reason Palestinians so violently resisted the early Jewish settlements is that they were *Jewish,* and the Palestinians were part of a people that had a long history of racism toward and oppression of Jews. Only by ignoring Palestinians' constantly repeated assertion that they were part of the larger Arab nation, and by ignoring the well-documented history of Arab oppression of Jews, can one think of Palestinians as innocent bystanders.

Given this history, the Palestinians can be understood as analogous in social position to American whites who today argue that affirmative action for African Americans unfairly punishes innocent whites. After all, the whites argue, we did not personally oppress Blacks, and in many cases, they can add, their white grandparents were themselves victims of discrimination or oppression in other lands. Furthermore, they had not even been living in the U.S. when slavery was imposed, and therefore they do not deserve blame for the consequences of slavery and racial oppression.

Those of us who support affirmative action argue that although there will be unintended victims who will be economically disadvantaged by affirmative action, they are not simply random victims, but rather people who benefit from the economic consequences of a system of racism and oppression, and therefore have to share some of the burdens when we seek to rectify the consequences of past wrongs. The logic of affirmative action makes it legitimate for some peoples to suffer the consequences for participating so long in a racist system of oppression toward Jews. Why the Palestinians? Because they happened to be living in the land from which the Jews had been unfairly and forcibly thrown out—land to which the Arab world prevented their return, and to which they had aspired to return from the moment they were first expelled.

Of course, one might reasonably argue here that if affirmative action is ever justified, it must be implemented with the greatest sensitivity to those who are going to be disadvantaged in the process. And that certainly did *not* happen. But the fault here can be apportioned equally on both sides. Palestinians were themselves easily manipulated by the large feudal landowning class of Arabs who feared that Jewish settlers, often espousing socialist ideas from their Eastern European leftist backgrounds, would incite the Arab masses to struggle against the exploitative class structure of the Islamic world. Through their control of the bazaars, the mosques, and the media, the Arab ruling elites did everything in their power to inflame tensions and racial hatred among the Arab masses toward the Jewish refugees who were coming to settle.

On the other hand, many Zionists did their part to inflame the situation. Had they encountered a European-style working class in Palestine, at least the socialists among them (and that was a very large segment) might have been inclined to consider forms of mutual cooperation. But a reactionary peasantry hardly seemed the basis for a class alliance. Moreover, many of the Zionists, including socialist Zionists, had been engaged in endless struggles in Europe for their right to Jewish self-determination and cultural and political autonomy. They had learned to organize Jewish trade unions and Jewish socialist institutions. They were Zionists in part because they had learned from the long history of attempts at living with their non-Jewish neighbors that these non-Jews could be counted on to turn upon and oppress Jews, and so Jews needed independent and autonomous institutions. Zionists created the early Jewish settlement (the Yishuv) in ways that would guarantee this Jewish autonomy and independence. Jewish trade unions, Jewish trade associations, and Jewish kibbutzim all excluded Arabs.

To an oppressed minority with a long history of being oppressed by their non-Jewish neighbors, such a form of organization made tremendous sense. Just as African Americans or women sometimes benefit from economic and political associations aimed primarily at giving them a voice, so the Jewish minority in Palestine felt the need for these kinds of exclusive organizations. Nevertheless, for the masses of Palestinian peasants who had lost their livelihoods and now had to find a new way to sell their labor, Jewish exclusivity in the major labor union (the Histadrut) had the additional effect of making it impossible for them to have any role in the emerging Jewish economy.

There were some Jews who understood these dynamics and tried to change the direction of the Yishuv in order to make it more sensitive to the needs of Palestinians. They were, for the most part, an isolated minority. The majority of Zionists doubted that there were

Demonstration of 50,000 Warsaw Jews protesting British restrictions on Jewish immigration to Palestine that were imposed to placate Arab nationalist and Palestinian sentiments.

any real possibilities for mutual cooperation with the Arab majority, and felt that their best hope was to build the infrastructure of what would eventually become an independent Jewish state. Those who sought to build alliances with Arabs found little support in the Arab world. The racist rhetoric toward Jews was matched with what often seemed an implacable resistance to any Jewish immigration into Palestine. As a result, Jews with the most progressive and antiracist attitudes could be dismissed as utopian idealists—even in the somewhat utopian context of early-twentieth-century Zionism.

When Jews Were the Refugees

The desperate need for a place of refuge from the anti-Semitism that dominated so much of the European and Islamic worlds took on a new immediacy for Jews with the growth of anti-Semitism in the late 1920s and 1930s. Yet at precisely this moment the world shut its doors to Jews. In no place was this ban on Jewish immigration felt more intensely than in Palestine—because the doors being shut here, so close to a Europe every day increasingly inflamed with Jew-hatred, were shut primarily in response to the demands of the Palestinian population. The British were far more responsive to the threats of oil-controlling Arab sheiks than to the pleas of Jewish refugees.

Imagine what we would say if the population of a northern state had succeeded in convincing the federal government to prohibit African Americans from the South from entering it. We could easily imagine the arguments, not fundamentally dissimilar to those used by the Arabs in the thirties: "These Blacks are going to set up their own society, will make it increasingly difficult for us whites to live in our cities, and will take over the culture and political life of our state. If you let them immigrate there will be no end to them, and they will eventually drive us out. We built these cities, we tilled the land in this state, and we don't want these others to come along and take it away from us."

We would reject this kind of argument in America, primarily because we understand the context of Black oppression. But certainly the level of oppression facing Jews, the active discrimination that would soon lead to the extermination camps, was greater still. To deny Jews entrance into Palestine, as the Palestinians succeeded in doing, was an act of unmatched racism and repression that would lead many Jews to feel all the more justified in their desire to obtain a state at any cost, and never to trust the Arabs.

To the Jews who managed to escape from the gas chambers and crematoria of Europe, Zionism was the one hope—a possibility that Jews would never again have to be dependent on the rather weak level of goodwill that non-Jews of the world had displayed during the Holocaust. But even after the facts of the Holocaust were revealed to the world, the Palestinian national movement stood resolute in its opposition to any accommodation with the Zionists, and insisted that the hundreds of thousands of Jews who had survived destruction should remain in displaced persons camps rather than be allowed to enter Palestine. Only the creation of the State of Israel in 1948 made it possible for the Jews to leave the camps and find a home. This callous disregard for Jewish survivors set the tone for a corresponding Jewish disregard for the fate of Palestinians who were displaced after 1948 by the Israeli War of Independence after.

The Creation of the State of Israel and the Palestinian Refugees

Given the history of oppression, the creation of the State of Israel was a modern-day miracle for the Jewish people. After close to two thousand years of being at the mercy of various "hosts" throughout the world, the Jewish people could finally claim a place of its own. We had every right to it, and we have every right to celebrate the creation of the State of Israel.

But this legitimate source of joy for the Jews became, quite tragically, a source of pain and suffering for the Palestinians.

I shall not attempt here to review all the excesses and abuse that the Israelis committed in the 1947–48 war to establish their state. The standard Zionist account—that Palestinians fled of their own free will at the behest of Arab leaders who felt that invading Arab armies would quickly destroy Israel—may account for a small portion of Arab refugees, but does not begin to acknowledge the role of Israelis in forcibly and systematically uprooting large groups of Palestinians who would have preferred to stay. As Benny Morris has shown in his essay "The New Historiography: Israel Confronts Its Past" (*Tikkun,* Volume 3, Number 6), from the mid-1930s most of the Yishuv's leaders, including Ben-Gurion, wanted to establish a Jewish state without an Arab minority or with as small an Arab minority as possible, and supported a "transfer solution." But the Yishuv did not enter the 1948 war with a master plan for expelling the Arabs, nor did its political and military leaders ever adopt such a master plan. There were Haganah/IDF expulsions of Arab communities, but there was no blanket policy of expulsions.

The Palestinian leadership rejected the various attempts at accommodation that the United Nations offered, particularly the offer in 1947 to divide the land into a Jewish state and a Palestinian state. It may well be true that some of the Zionist leaders who embraced the partition offer of 1947 thought that, at some future date, they would be able to expand the borders of the Israeli state. But their openness to partition amounted to recognition, in principle, of the validity of Palestinian national self-determination. The Palestinian leadership's willingness to risk all and then to lose all in order to prevent the Jews from achieving a state of their own was an indication of how deep their hatred and how determined their opposition was to Jewish national self-determination.

Most of those who suffered as a result of this irresponsible and immoral leadership were Palestinian peasants and small-time merchants who had no real understanding of what their leaders were doing in their name, no democratic mechanisms to influence them, and no way of knowing about the history or contemporary fate of the Jewish people. While most of the Palestinians had come to believe that their existence as a people was being threatened by Jewish immigration—a belief that seemed to be confirmed by the creation of a huge Palestinian refugee population in 1948—there was no real mechanism for those who might have sought peaceful accommodation to express their views or to make themselves known to the many Israelis who also hoped for a peaceful reconciliation between the two peoples.

The Palestinian people had become the tragic victims of a historical process for which, as part of the Islamic people that had historically oppressed Jews, they were not entirely guilt-free, but for which they also were not entirely responsible. Conversely, the Jews of Europe were victims of nineteen hundred years of Christian anti-Semitism—anti-Semitism that had been reinforced and made to seem "the way of the world" by a corresponding history of oppression and discrimination for hundreds of years in Arab lands. Their leap from the burning building of Europe caused them to land on the backs of the Palestinians. They did not jump *in order* to hurt Palestinians, and certainly not in order to become junior partners with European colonialists. Nevertheless, the conditions of oppression they had faced made them incapable of showing appropriate caring for those on whose backs they had fallen, incapable of recognizing that they were causing pain and suffering to others, and incapable of seeing themselves as both victims and victimizers.

As a result of this insensitivity, the jump from the burning building of Europe caused more pain and more suffering than it had to. The Israeli population has never fully acknowledged the consequences of that original jump—the creation of a Palestinian refugee population living in UN camps in Arab lands. On the contrary, the Israelis have locked themselves into a pattern of denial, unable to imagine that those who hate them today have any possible justification other than the irrational hatred that has always governed the way non-Jews treat Jews. Yet this inability on the part of Israelis to see their situation clearly is a disability for Jews. It keeps Israel in a situation that makes its existence more precarious; it is *not* a manifestation of strength and self-interest, but of neurosis and paralysis. This neurosis is the price that the world continues to pay today for having done so little in the course of the past nineteen hundred years to combat the systematic oppression of Jews in European and Islamic lands.

The Zionism-is-Racism Slander

In 1991 the United Nations rescinded a resolution declaring that "Zionism is racism." The account here should show how ridiculous it was to try to describe the complex circumstances under which the Jewish national liberation struggle was fought as merely a manifestation of racism or colonialism. In the face of systematic genocide, the Jews chose Zionism as the vehicle for national liberation. Like every national liberation movement, Zionism was distorted by the conditions under which it emerged and under which it had to fight. But once one knows the details of the story, it is impossible to argue that Zionism is simply a manifestation of colonialism, or is essentially a racist movement.

Those who claim that "Zionism is racism" refer to the fact that once Israel was set up, it gave special privileges to Jews over Arabs. The Law of Return gave rights to Jews that it did not give to others, and in general the allocation of resources in the state has tended to be governed by an unfair principle that privileges Jews.

But creating a society that advantages one group over others is not necessarily racist. Rather, Israel is the first example of what later became an accepted principle of affirmative action to rectify the consequences of previous discrimination. The world systematically oppressed or allowed others to oppress and murder the Jews; eventually it realized that this was wrong and allowed for the creation of the State of Israel to rectify past wrongs. It is sometimes appropriate to give priority in allocation of resources to a previously disadvantaged group, even if another group is disadvantaged in the process.

There are moments when this process can go too far. That, for example, is the contention of many people in the U.S. today about affirmative action in relationship to African Americans—that it has gone too far and disadvantaged too many innocent bystanders. Though such a contention is worthy of serious consideration, it merits more consideration if it is raised by those who acknowledge the original wrong and acknowledge the validity of the initial attempts at affirmative action; less when it is raised by those who did the oppressing in the first place and who never acknowledged the validity of attempting to redress the wrongs. The same reasoning should be applied to the State of Israel: Claims that the disadvantaging of Arabs may have gone too far should be seriously considered, but they deserve more attention when raised by those who acknowledge the original oppression of the Jewish people, including the oppression they faced in Arab lands, and recognize the right of the world to set up a state that disproportionately favors Jews to attempt to rectify past injustices.

On the other hand, those who never acknowledged the right of Israel to exist, or who think that affirmative action for Jews is racist, may themselves be revealing insensitivity toward the Jewish people that bespeaks their own racism. Since many of the peoples of the world acted in a racist manner toward the Jews in the past (e.g., the Palestinians denied them the right to immigrate during the Holocaust), their current judgments must be very carefully questioned.

Once one begins to ask the right questions, one sees a double standard that is the hallmark of racist attitudes: Israel's oppressive policies have been singled out from the oppressive policies of most of the rest of the nations of the world, and subjected to special condemnation not accorded to others. This is not to say that if everyone does it, it's OK. But in this case, suspicions of worldwide racism toward the

Jews seem to be confirmed by the United Nations' "Zionism-is-racism" resolution.

There are other, more concrete explanations for why the "Zionism-is-racism" formula caught on and originally found legitimation in the United Nations. First, since 1967, many countries have been quite reasonably angry about the ongoing oppression of Palestinians caused by the Israeli occupation of the West Bank and Gaza. Legitimate anger at the Occupation sets the stage for attacks on Israel that may then lead beyond the boundaries of legitimate criticism. Second, the economic power of the oil-producing states leads many Third World nations to wish to secure their status in the eyes of these states. Third, as happened during the Gulf War, there is the desire to strike out at the United States, which can be acted out symbolically by attacking Israel, an American ally. Fourth, there is the abiding anger in the Third World at all forms of colonialism, and the formation of Israel is understood as a colonial phenomenon. All of these factors certainly played a role in the original UN resolution. Nevertheless, the decision to single out Israel is striking because many of the countries that voted for the resolution are themselves guilty of far more serious human-rights violations than anything the Israelis have done. The passage of this resolution is one of the great instances of hypocrisy in the postwar period. Its ultimate consequence was to undermine the credibility of the United Nations as a moral force—and it is only as a moral force that the General Assembly has had any power to influence world events. Nor did that moral force gain much credibility when the resolution was finally rescinded in 1991. At that time, UN members seemed far more interested in pleasing a United States that had emerged as the world's undisputed superpower (after the collapse of the Soviet Union and the military defeat of Iraq) than in seriously grappling with the moral distortions inherent in the resolution that it was now dutifully rescinding.

If one uses a double standard to judge a particular group harshly, and if that group just happens to be the same group that has been subject to a long and unabated history of racism and oppression, it is reasonable to suspect that the unfair judgment being made of that group is itself racist.

But before we dismiss the "Zionism-is-racism" position entirely, we should acknowledge that there are some principled internationalists—people who actually believe and consistently support the position that *every* form of nationalism, and hence every national liberation struggle, is a form of racism that unfairly privileges one particular national, ethnic, or religious tradition over another. They actively oppose every form of nationalism equally. For such a person, the position that Zionism is racism need not be anti-Semitic, if in fact, in their actual practice, they are giving as much energy to attacking Cuban, Chinese, African American, Irish, Polish, Norwegian, Australian, Canadian, Mexican, French, Egyptian, Syrian, Iraqi, Japanese, American, Vietnamese, and Balinese nationalisms as they are giving to attacking Zionism. There are very few such people. All too often, those leftists who hide behind the notion of being opposed to all nationalisms in fact give a disproportionate amount of their energy to publicly opposing Zionism—and that *is* a strong indication of anti-Semitism.

Haredi Anti-Zionism

Just as a certain kind of principled antinationalism, when applied universally with equal fervor, can lead to an anti-Zionism that is *not* anti-Semitic, so too there is an anti-Zionism that emerges from the Jewish religious tradition. Some of the haredim, the so-called ultra-Orthodox, are religiously opposed to Zionism. These haredim believe that the attempt to rebuild a Jewish state substitutes human action for divine, and that such attempts are necessarily sinful and likely to lead in a disastrous direction. Many of these people took a similar approach to the Holocaust and to other events in Jewish history, seeing them as punishments from God for not fulfilling God's will. Many haredim felt it would have been useless to organize resistance to the Nazis, and many of their community were led "like sheep to the slaughter" during the Holocaust.

One might argue that the perspective of the haredim is the classic internalization of self-blame that has affected the victimized throughout history. Similarly, one might adopt the Zionist perspective and argue that this passivity and inability to claim one's potential role in shaping history is the specific and inevitable result of being an oppressed group in the Diaspora—the very Diaspora-neurosis that Zionism is meant to cure. One might even argue that this kind of theological perspective is mixed with an intense degree of self-hatred and self-denigration. All these arguments may have some validity, but they do not prove that the essence of the position is Jew-hatred. The haredi position has a legitimacy within the Jewish dialogue that cannot be so easily dismissed, particularly in light of the actual outcome of Israel's current political practice. However, its legitimacy depends on accepting the entire framework of its reasoning, its roots in a strong religious conception of God's role in history, and a consistent willingness to suspend one's own will and to rely on what one takes to be God's will. Anti-Zionists who detach this specific idea from the rest of the framework of haredi belief cannot cite it to prove that non-haredim who hold this position are doing so in a non-anti-Semitic way.

Legitimate Criticism

There are several areas in which Israel can rightly be criticized. First, in the creation of the State of Israel, between six hundred thousand and one million Arabs were forcefully displaced. This was a terrible consequence of the creation of the State. The Jewish people have never fully acknowledged this unintended evil for which we were partially responsible, and the State of Israel has never taken any serious steps to consider what it ought to do to compensate the Palestinians for the pain they experienced. This criticism is important, particularly if it is not overstated or used as proof of the fundamentally "evil" or "racist" character of the State of Israel. We certainly ought to remember that the creation of refugee populations, particularly in the years after World War II, was a common phenomenon. Millions of Muslims were displaced and many murdered in the creation of India and Pakistan in 1947. Yet the resultant population transfers, never democratically agreed to by the people who were thus affected, have not been condemned as evidence that Indian nationalism simply *is* racism.

Second, Israel continues to oppress and occupy the lands of Palestinians in the wake of the 1967 war. Israelis are correct to point out that the world did not similarly protest when Jordan occupied the Palestinian lands in the period between 1948 and 1967. Nevertheless, it is still appropriate to condemn the current Occupation and to insist that Israel allow Palestinian national self-determination, if that can be achieved—as I believe it can—in ways that would protect Israeli survival. We at *Tikkun* and those in our public education arm, the Committee for Judaism and Social Justice, have repeatedly protested Israeli policy toward the Palestinians.

Zionism can be Consistent with a Palestinian State

The Zionist ideal of a state in the ancient homeland of the Jewish people does not necessarily conflict with the aspiration of Palestinians for national self-determination. Leading members of the Israeli military establishment, including many retired Israeli generals, have outlined a plan for a "Two State Solution" that would provide adequate security for Israel while allowing Palestinians the dignity and independence that they seek.

A two state solution would require Israel to give up control of the West Bank and Gaza and cede land for a highway through the Negev connecting the two parts of this state. It would require Palestinians to accept total demilitarization by preventing the introduction of any armaments into the state of Palestine.

When Israel originally agreed to the UN partition plan, it did not demand demilitarization of the Palestinian state. But after Palestinians joined the Arab states in trying to eliminate the State of Israel in 1948, and subsequently wrote into the charter of the PLO a call for the total dismantling of Israel, and after decades of terrorism against Jewish civilians by the PLO, Jews are not being paranoid or unreasonable to demand that if a Palestinian state is formed it be demilitarized (just as Germany, Japan, and Austria were demilitarized after WWII). While we should work for total demilitarization of the entire region (including Israel) and of the entire world, it is no act of friendship to the Palestinians to ask them to wait for a state until the Israeli population feels ready to live with a Palestinian army on its borders. And while some American radicals think that such a demand is unfair, most Palestinians in the West Bank would be very happy to accept a state under such conditions.

The actual practical outcome of Zionism has been hurtful to the Palestinians. But so too has the practical outcome of socialist ideas, as manifested in Eastern Europe, been even more hurtful to tens of millions of people. The key in both cases is that the distortions do not necessarily flow from the ideal, but from the misuse of those ideals in specific historical circumstances. Just as we don't want to throw out the ideals of the left because of the actual history of the Soviet Union that professed left ideals, so we don't want to discard or fundamentally discredit Zionism just because Zionist ideals were sometimes used in an oppressive way.

5

The Denial of Anti-Semitism
in the Contemporary World

Most contemporary instances of anti-Zionism are anti-Semitic, although we've been careful to describe some circumstances under which they are not. Given the long history of oppression of the Jews and the recurrence with which anti-Semitism seems to infect the collective unconscious of significant parts of the world, it is not surprising that, with a few exceptions, attacks on Zionism have also displayed a disturbing strain of anti-Semitism.

The same argument applies to other groups and opposition to their liberation struggles. While one might, for example, oppose some specific tactics of the Black liberation movement, that does not justify opposing the entire concept of Black liberation, and finding it racist because its fulfillment would necessarily involve disadvantaging some whites. We might suspect that those who are making this argument are expressing their own racism and (conscious or unconscious) hatred of Blacks. When making critical judgements about a liberation struggle of an oppressed minority, the burden of proof falls on those who have grown up within a racist culture and have benefited from it, not on the oppressed group.

Most Americans who paid attention to the arguments about affirmative action for Blacks and women in the 1960s and 1970s probably understand this concept when it applies to these two groups. Why don't they understand it as applied to Jews? Similarly, they are very quick to recognize instances of racism and code words that imply negative views about Blacks. Why is there no similar sensitivity toward Jews?

Or, to put it another way, why haven't the most sensitive people in our society taken anti-Semitism more seriously?

Why Didn't Americans Ever Seriously Address Anti-Semitism?

Before answering this question, let's first look at what actually happened. Before World War II, anti-Semitism was explicitly articulated through many sections of American society and even more explicitly articulated in other Western societies. Jews faced a quota system that excluded them from many jobs, businesses, universities, country clubs, and positions of political and social power.

Although most Americans consciously rejected the Jew-hating that was at the center of the anti-Semitic agenda, they tended to accept many of the assumptions about Jews that were part of that agenda. This included such beliefs as: "The Jews killed Christ, and their descendents continue to deserve punishment for that crime"; "the Jews are Communists and threaten our society"; "the Jews are the capitalists who control our society"; "the Jews have an international conspiracy to control the world and have more power than everyone else"; "the Jews are spineless and will never fight for anything they believe in"; "the Jews are more materialistic than others and can't be trusted"; "the Jews are smarter and better able to manipulate than others and can't be trusted"; "the Jews are more sexually liberated and obsessed with sex than others"; "the Jews are more rigid and less loving than others"; "the Jews just care about abstract justice but don't care about mercy"; "the Jews are more sensitive than others"; "the Jews are less sensitive than others"; or "Jews are really not like others."

Until the start of World War II it was possible to hear these and other stereotypical assumptions about Jews articulated by intelligent people in "polite society." But once the U.S. got involved in the war, for reasons that had little to do with saving the Jews, Nazi anti-Semitism became one of the issues used by the U.S. government and media to deepen support for the war effort. Consequently, it became *unpatriotic* to be anti-Semitic. Anti-Semitism was a sign that you were on the other side—perhaps a traitor—and hence it was officially

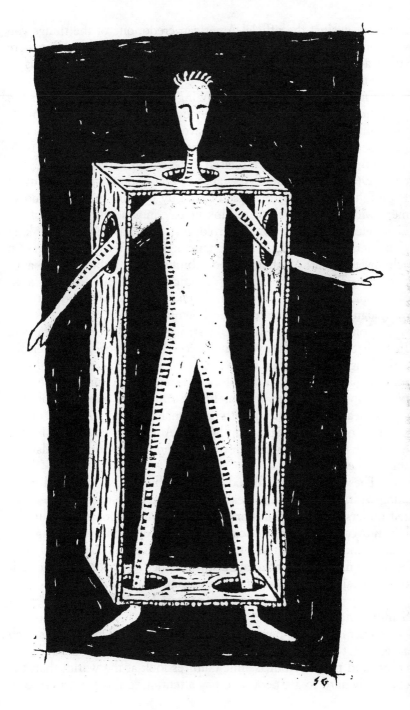

opposed, against the official American credo, one of the things you were not supposed to support if you were a *real* American. But there still wasn't any serious confrontation with the ideological basis of anti-Semitism.

One obstacle to such a rethinking of anti-Semitic ideas was the prominent role of the various branches of Christianity. For example, the Catholic Church would never have allowed a public examination of those parts of its own teachings that had generated anti-Semitism. When the Catholic Church revised its teachings at the Vatican Council in 1963, it did so largely because of the wisdom and humanity of Pope John XXIII, not because of a vastly popular grassroots movement within the church to rethink its role in generating some of the ideological conditions for the Holocaust. Nor has such a rethinking characterized most of the Protestant denominations—much less an acknowledgment of their responsibility for the history of anti-Semitism. The churches may issue official statements rejecting anti-Semitism, but they rarely undertake any serious educational campaign to confront or refute anti-Semitic ideas.

Contrast this with the public struggle against sexism or racism. In both cases, these movements succeeded in provoking a serious rethinking of the entire history of race or sexual relations. Many Americans have rejected the Black or feminist account of those relations, but few educated and intelligent Americans have been able to escape hearing and dealing with these analyses. And while still only a minority of the population, millions of Americans have been forced to rethink themselves and their own lives and assumptions in relationship to these issues.

These movements forced precisely this kind of personal grappling with the issues and "dealing with" the challenges to one's own self-understanding. An important segment of opinion-shapers in the U.S. moved from being officially opposed to discrimination against women and Blacks—willing to articulate such a position publicly—to being genuinely concerned about these issues and ready to make serious societal changes to right the wrongs.

Why did this kind of "working through" or "dealing with" anti-Semitism never take place?

There are three parts to the answer. First, anti-Semitism is such a deep part of the culture, so thoroughly ingrained in the way Westerners and people from Islamic cultures look at the world, that it is extremely hard to get people to pay attention to this particular form of hatred. But, one might object, so are sexism and hatred of Blacks. True; so to understand why those forms of hatred *were* dealt with and anti-Semitism not, we need to add two additional parts to the answer.

The second part is that women and Blacks *insisted* that their oppression be dealt with in the public arena, while those who act as official spokespeople for the Jewish community have always shied away from such a demand—in part because of a deeply held anti-goyish sentiment that leads many Jews to believe that the non-Jew will "never get it" and that the only way to deal with anti-Semitism is to have a strong Israel. Moreover, many of these leaders are assimilationists who instinctively believe that the best way for Jews to behave is to keep a low profile, not offend anyone, and struggle only for one thing—Israeli military security.

Moreover, it is not clear that if Jews *did* demand that their oppression be dealt with, people would listen. White Americans confronted Black oppression only when faced with public protests and demonstrations that created a climate of urgency. Similarly, it was the ability of women to confront men in families and personal relationships that gave them the social power to force their issue onto the public agenda in a way that made it necessary for men to rethink these issues.

Of course, it would be foolish to overestimate the social power of women or Blacks—the fact is that they have *not* had sufficient power to stop the oppression they face. Nor have most people been completely successful in uprooting their own biases and oppressive behaviors. But most reasonably aware people have rethought their relationship to these issues and confronted, at least intellectually, the analysis put forth by the spokespeople of these liberation movements.

Jews, on the other hand, do not have this kind of social power. The social power often attributed to Jews is that of having attained positions of influence in the media and the educational and professional arenas. But this power has been attained primarily by Jews who have accepted the assimilationist thesis that their own advances require them to play down their Jewishness, and that their own successes prove that Jews can make it and find security to the extent that they play by non-Jewish rules. They believe that they have whatever social power they have precisely and solely to the extent that they don't make an issue of their Jewishness. These are the people who donate money to a non-elected "leadership" of establishment Jewish organizations—which, in turn, propose defending Jewish interests primarily by supporting Israel and secondarily by remembering the Holocaust and fighting only the most extreme forms of anti-Semitism.

Many Jewish organizations rarely fight the more deeply ingrained anti-Semitism that is part of the collective unconscious of Western society. Their deep pessimism about non-Jews, expressed inside the Jewish world in a pervasive "goyim-bashing," discourages them from even beginning a full-scale assault on anti-Semitism. Instead, all they ask is that non-Jews give Israel enough support so that there will be a place to escape to when these non-Jews turn on them. And precisely because of their conviction of the need to find such a haven, they are reluctant to offer any criticism of Israel's current policies, and are unable to see that Israel would actually be stronger and more secure if it were perceived as doing its best to achieve justice for Palestinians. Jewish pessimism runs so deep that many of these Jewish organizations believe that no matter what Israel does, everyone will be against it—allowing them to justify Israeli policies that do not even attempt to recognize the validity of a Palestinian right to national self-determination. A people so frightened that it acts self-destructively, and so fearful of non-Jews that it can't persuade them to act as allies even when they might be willing (and they won't always be), is a people too scared and too scarred to fight effectively the more subtle forms of anti-Semitism that currently flourish in American society.

Paradoxically, this deep fear of non-Jews prevents those Jews who *do* have some limited social power from pressing for a public confrontation with anti-Semitism except of the most gross and isolated kind (explicit Nazism or acts of violence against Jews). In short, one reason the public consciousness has never fully addressed anti-Semitism is the real and surplus powerlessness of the Jews.

But there is a third part of the answer. In the case of women and Blacks, it was only a few years from the moment these groups insisted on the importance of their liberation struggles to the moment they became central parts of the litany of issues and demands of the Left. This help was central in legitimating the demand for a societal rethinking of these issues. But the Left has steadfastly refused to acknowledge that anti-Semitism deserves a societal focus. Without that legitimation, Jews who *have* raised this issue have been portrayed as being narrowly sectarian and self-interested, rather than as crusaders for a cause that the society has unfairly neglected.

The Specificity of Anti-Semitism

The Jewish community was so traumatized by the Holocaust that it never fully faced the question of what in the peculiar structure of Jewish oppression had led to it. Instead, many Jews reverted to one of two possible simplistic explanations. One was that the irredeemable untrustworthiness of the non-Jew had reasserted itself. (Solution: Found a Jewish state, make it strong, and be prepared to leave at any moment for that safe haven.) The other was that some evil force or sickness had overtaken the German people (there was some debate about whether this was endemic to German character-structure and culture or a temporary phenomenon), but now those with the sickness had been killed, jailed, or magically cured—in any case, it was no longer a serious problem. According to the second argument, we could go on supporting the cold war and align ourselves with the now-cured Germans. We could stop worrying about anti-Semitism except as some irrational and unpredictable evil (perhaps a manifestation of original sin, or of a Freudian death wish, or Thanatos) that might reappear at any moment (because who can control evil anyway?), but against which nothing could be done but to prepare oneself for a world that is fatally flawed in ways that would inevitably produce limits on human perfectibility, limits on any liberal reformist ideas, and limits on any program to achieve a peaceful and mutually cooperative world.

Together, these two ideas produced a form of Jewish neo-conservatism that held that American power must be supported so that America would defend Israel militarily (in other words, full support for American imperial adventures in exchange for an alliance with Israel). There is no point in trying to restructure or heal the problems that cause people to accept fascist solutions, neo-conservatives argued, because, in any event, their fundamental evil or death wish will allow fascism to triumph regardless of how much radical restructuring is attempted.

This kind of picture helped Jews fit in with the psychological dynamics of postwar America. If evil is ontologized or made into a permanent feature of reality, one need not look at the details of one's own society to see which of its qualities might make the triumph of evil more or less likely. Ironically, then, mainstream American-Jewish Holocaust obsession often helped people avoid seriously grappling with the Holocaust. The Holocaust became rooted in forces of evil that were either outside rational control or built into everyone's psyche equally. In either case, it no longer required people to reflect on the economic and social realities that allowed Hitler to triumph and the Jews to be scapegoated.

What such accounts necessarily avoid is the specific form of Jewish oppression. To review the argument of this book:

Jews were targeted both because of the revolutionary anti-authoritarian thrust of Judaism, with its implicit challenge to every ruling class, and because Jews had known and rejected Jesus and Muhammad. But in addition to that—both as a consequence of past oppression and a guarantor of future vulnerability—Jews were historically given the opportunities, skills, and economic necessity of serving in positions where, by the nature of the jobs, they served as the public face of the ruling classes, exerting powers over others and sometimes being the vehicle for the oppression of the larger system. Whether as the agents of East European landowners, shopkeepers, business leaders, foremen, tax collectors, pawnbrokers, moneylenders, lawyers, doctors, teachers, psychologists, social workers, or government bureaucrats, Jews were (and are) often in the position of appearing to have power over others, even though, by and large, they were serving the economic and political interests of others. In fact, Jews have not been the major decision makers inside the banks and corporations that have shaped Western imperial directions.

Jews were not in a position to exercise decisive power to save themselves from the Holocaust, or to persuade the governments of Western countries to bomb the concentration camps and railroads leading to the concentration camps—much less to get the U.S. to enter the war against Hitler before it was directly attacked at Pearl Harbor. If Jews had had *real* power, and not just the power that comes from being accessories, advisors, and intermediaries to those with real power, they would have been in a position to interfere with the systematic destruction of the Jewish people during World War II—a fact that was well-known to Jews throughout the world by 1943.

Jews have been systematically set up in intermediate positions between those with real power and those without. Jews appear to have power, and hence are a convenient locus of anger when the pain caused by the social system becomes acute for people on the lower rungs.

Because Jews are placed in positions where they can serve as the focus for anger that might otherwise be directed at ruling elites,

no matter how much economic security or political influence individual Jews may achieve, they can never be sure that they will not once again become the targets of popular attack should the society in which they live enter periods of severe economic strain or political conflict.

It is precisely this hidden vulnerability that constitutes the uniqueness of Jewish oppression.

Because of past exclusion from owning or working the land—as well as the inner cultural dynamics of Jewish tradition—intellectual work and selling goods became skills that Jews developed for survival. These skills gave Jews a comparative advantage when entering a level playing field, so that Jews were more likely than the average person to succeed in getting into intermediate positions of power. We should not pretend that Jews have typically *experienced* this societal position as oppressive. On the contrary, compared to the situation of most working people, these "intermediary" positions have often seemed to Jews to be positions of special privilege, and Jews have often been grateful to kings, queens, landed gentry, or capitalist ruling elites who have given them this opportunity. Rarely recognizing the double-edged nature of the deal, many Jews have done their best to get into these positions, enjoyed the rewards, and looked askance at anyone who then suggested that there might be a hidden cost to holding these positions.

In capitalist societies, mobility from working-class to ruling-class positions is very limited, but there are often opportunities for some sections of the working class to move up the ladder to positions in the middle and professional classes (depending on the specific case—less so when there are depressions, more so when there are periods of steady economic growth). Jewish cultural advantages have helped put Jews in these positions, and it is precisely in these positions that they are vulnerable *as a group*. **August Bebel put it brilliantly when he termed anti-Semitism the "socialism of fools." That is, anti-Semitism in the contemporary period has as one important root people's resentment of their oppression in daily life. This resentment is then directed toward one of the recognizable agents of the oppressors rather than at the oppressors themselves.**

Compounding the picture are the psychological dynamics of modern nationalism. Modern nationalism emerged in societies that had been touched by the promise of capitalism, but who had been unable to fulfill that promise for the majority of its citizens. The original promise of capitalism and the bourgeois revolutions was to create a society of liberty, fraternity, and equality. In fact, they created societies of intense class divisions from which a small group of people benefited disproportionately. Liberty, for most, became the liberty to sell their labor power to the owners of the means of production; equality became the equal opportunity to compete for scarce jobs; and fraternity seemed particularly difficult to come by the more the society encouraged the competitive ethos of the marketplace. Class divisions threatened to tear these societies apart during much of the nineteenth century, but they were mitigated in the most powerful capitalist societies by the dynamics of imperialism. The capitalist societies that were strongest economically and militarily were able to establish direct rule colonies or, after World War II, indirect rule of client states; they thereby created favorable conditions for trade that allowed the wealth of these Third World countries to be brought home to the colonial or imperial center.

Colonial powers shaped the Third World economies in ways that undermined their self-sufficiency and tied them irrevocably to an international market whose prices the colonial or imperial powers set. Through the gradual immiseration of these Third World countries advanced capitalist societies could offset the worst economic consequences of the internal class struggle. The colonies would continue to generate a certain amount of wealth that could be distributed to the domestic working classes. This colonial system worked well for the most powerful states (France and Britain were able to divide much of Africa and Asia; the Monroe Doctrine claimed United States hegemony over all of Central and South America), but led to conflict once the developing capitalist states (Germany, Italy, Japan) began competing for these markets. The later developing capitalist states wanted a cut, and felt angered and oppressed by a division of the world's resources that gave them no way of using colonialist expansion to relieve the internal class divisions and conflict that always arise when one has unequal distribution of wealth and power. Nationalism is, in part, the public expression of the self-interest of these various societies engaged in a worldwide struggle for economic benefits that will relieve internal tensions.

Yet nationalism is not merely a manifestation of rational self-interest, but often builds on a fantasized image of the nation as the embodiment of one's greatest hopes for a community of meaning that is painfully absent in the daily experience of most people. It is not solely economic oppression that drives people to anger at their lives in capitalist society, but also and importantly the deprivation of meaning, the absence of fraternity, and the sense that they are in constant competition and struggle when most human beings really want to be supportive and loving with others. Since the realities of daily life do not provide that kind of supportive and loving connection, and do not provide a framework of meaning in which one can see one's personal life as part of an ethically and spiritually meaningful whole, people are driven to find other sources of meaning that somehow transcend their daily lives and give them purpose. The two major contenders for that source of meaning in the past two hundred years have been religion and nationalism.

Nationalism has often functioned as the illusory community through which individuals imagine themselves connected to one another when the competitive marketplace and their stressful and alienated jobs don't give them that real connection. Nationalism gives their lives meaning to the extent that it contributes to this larger whole. But no matter how powerful the music and the poetry, the art and the spectacle, the literature and the marching bands, in the end, people return to a daily life that still fails to fulfill them.

Why don't these substitute pseudocommunities provide the fulfillment people seek? The answer is that real community can work only if the structures of daily life are themselves changed, so that people are given real power in their work world to create a reality that allows for real connection, real fraternity, and real ability to actualize their human capacities. Yet this answer is strongly resisted by the wealthy and powerful elites who stand to lose everything if the economy is radically remade to serve human needs. So they provide another answer, one that has strong resonance in the history of anti-Semitism: There is some "Other"—some group that is not "us," that is depriving the rest of us of what we need to have a more fulfilling life. Nationalism claims it can meet people's need for meaning if it can subjugate or eliminate this dangerous Other. Of course, it is not only the Jews who have played the role of the "other": in virtually every society where a ruling elite has needed to establish its power, it has found this Other to hate. But in the West it has overwhelmingly and consistently been the Jews who have most frequently been identified as this subversive Other through most of the past two thousand years.

Once a particular group becomes the target of choice for a particular nationalism, the officially identified "evil Other," the hatred of this group takes on a life of its own, becomes a major factor in the communal life of a society, and can no longer be totally reduced to the factors that cause it. For example, the Nazis diverted energies from their war effort against the Russian Army in order to pursue their war against the Jews more successfully. Anti-Semitism had taken on such a life of its own that any attempt to remedy it would have required *both* transforming the societal dynamics that generated the need for this evil Other *and* systematically uprooting ideological and emotional commitments to Jew-hating.

The Holocaust is less mysterious when we think about it in these terms. Instead of attributing it to the unique distortions of German culture, to the irrevocable evil in the non-Jew, to the mysterious ability of evil to erupt in human beings who are otherwise contained and sane, or to some other inexplicable or irrational force or sickness, we can now understand the Holocaust as the working out of dynamics that are deeply rooted in the normal operations of Western society, but usually do not manifest themselves in this kind of explicit campaign of extermination. Yet as long as the society has identified an evil Other and sustained racist consciousness, it will always be ready to move to more extreme forms of racist oppression should that society face deep inner conflict and uncertainty. Every class society needs to build this kind of racist safety valve for its ruling class.

It is not surprising that American Jews, the biggest population of Jews who had survived the various attempts in this century to wipe out the Jewish people, would not want to face this problem squarely. To face this situation of vulnerability would require questioning the entire class structure and all forms of contemporary nationalism. Under normal conditions, that class structure allows Jews to have temporary advantage when a society is functioning well—so why think about what happens when things aren't going well? After World War II, Jews were faced with an opportunity to "make it" in Western societies. Why bite the hand that was feeding them? Fully confronting anti-Semitism would force the Jewish people to challenge the class dynamics of the capitalist world, to challenge the imperial system, and to challenge the psychodynamics of contemporary nationalism. American nationalism had just been used to fight the Nazis, so it was easier to believe that only German nationalism could be turned against the Jews, to imagine that there was something specific to German historical realities that created this dynamic, and to avoid facing the possibility that all nationalisms typically call for some evil Other as potential victim.

To the extent that anyone was raising these questions, it tended to be Old Leftists, who thought that the solution was simply to eliminate capitalism, who would not acknowledge the reality of anti-Semitism in the Soviet Union or in the Left, and who had no commitment to fighting anti-Semitism. What Jew would want to align herself or himself with a Marxist analysis that seemed relatively discredited by the actual behavior of the leftists themselves? And who would want to confront American capitalism at the very moment that it seemed to have defeated the Nazi threat? It is not hard to under-

stand why a group that had just barely survived a massive attempt to exterminate it would not be itching for a new fight—particularly against those who had sheltered it.

So instead, there was a massive denial of what could have been the lessons of the Holocaust. Rather than question the arrangement that both gave them opportunities to make it and also set them in positions that in the long run might lead to a resurgence of anti-Jewish impulses on the part of the oppressed, the Jewish world set off to memorialize the victims and build the State of Israel as an escape from the resurgence of anti-Semitism that many believed would be inevitable.

This compromise that the Jews struck with their own history created a generalized paranoia—a sense that no one could ever be trusted. Yet since the Jews would not allow themselves to face and confront what was rational about these fears—the *actual* structure of Jewish oppression—the fears had to appear, both to themselves and others, as the product of a generalized "goyim-bashing" that won neither friends nor allies. They could not allow themselves to know the legitimate basis of their fears, but neither could they feel secure.

Jewish fears may be justified—not because non-Jews can't be trusted, but because the structure of Jewish oppression puts us into a very vulnerable position in society, a position that becomes much more precarious to the extent that a deep social crisis emerges. But since Jews don't understand the reasons why their fears are justified, they are unable to explain them to others except in terms that sound offensive or paranoid ("we can never trust the non-Jews").

6
The Left's Denial of Anti-Semitism in Postwar America

It's not hard to understand why the mainstream American Left in the postwar period did not give major focus to anti-Semitism. Most of that Left—with the notable exception of relatively small and ineffective leftovers from the Trotskyite and democratic-socialist traditions—was still committed to supporting and defending a Soviet Union now under the threat of an escalating cold war, and also to defending itself from the witch-hunts that culminated in McCarthyism. In other words, to focus on the vicious anti-Semitism that was manifested in Stalin's fabrication of a "Jewish doctors' plot" and that persisted in the Soviet Union throughout the post-Stalinist decades might only add fuel to already burning anti-Soviet feeling in the U.S. It never occurred to many of these activists of the Old Left that by telling the truth about the Left and about the Soviet Union, they could have gained their greatest credibility in the eyes of many who had come to suspect that the "truth" being told by the Left was at least as distorted as the "truth" being told by the capitalist-controlled Western media.

But why did the New Left that emerged in the 1960s, itself committed to rejecting the Communist party, the Soviet Union, and much of the substance and style of the Old Left, similarly avoid and deny the problem of anti-Semitism?

Many in the New Left thought that anti-Semitism was no longer a problem, and that it had simply been defeated along with Hitler in

71

World War II. But what rational person who bothered to inquire into the history of anti-Semitism could possibly have held that position? Would anyone who held an analogous position about racism toward Blacks after schools had been integrated in the South and all forms of legal segregation declared illegal have been deemed credible? Would anyone on the Left have given credibility to the notion that racism was defeated once the Civil Rights Bill of 1964 had been passed?

Was there any evidence that anti-Semitic ideas had now been extinguished from the dialogue of civilized humanity? What about the overt use of anti-Semitism in the language of the Communist party elites who purged Jews from the leadership of the Polish Communist party in 1956? What about the continued suppression of Jewish rights in the Soviet Union? What about the willingness of Western countries, particularly the U.S., to recredit former Nazis for use in the anti-Communist crusade? What about the prevalence of Jews among those blacklisted in the McCarthyism of the 1950s? What about the use of explicit anti-Semitic stereotypes and fascist literature in the education of the youth of many Arab countries—not to mention their loudly proclaimed desire to "push the Jews into the sea"? Perhaps all these might have been relatively light matters if they stood alone; but how could they reasonably be treated that way by a world that had just endured and to some extent cooperated with the extermination of one out of every three Jews?

> Is it reasonable to imagine that, had there been such a genocide against another of America's ethnic groups forty or fifty years ago, the New Left would have given it as little attention as it gave anti-Semitism? No.

So why did this happen in the New Left of the 1960s, 1970s, 1980s, and 1990s?

To answer this question, we need to look at the psychology of Jews on the Left who would have needed to take the lead in raising this issue (just as it was a movement of African Americans that forced a consciousness of racism and a movement of women that forced a consciousness of sexism). But these Jewish New Leftists had little understanding of the history or specific form taken by contemporary versions of anti-Jewish racism. Just as Jewish vulnerability had been incomprehensible to the prosperous and successful Jews of Weimar Germany, so it was beyond the categories of American New Leftists.

The Failure of the New Left to Grasp the Dynamics of Anti-Semitism

In the immediate postwar years, many American Jews made dramatic economic advances. No wonder, then, that younger Jews growing up in the postwar period had a hard time making sense of their parents' fears. They could sympathize with the pain their elders had experienced in the Holocaust; they could share the anger at the Nazis; and they could share the determination "never again" to allow anything of this sort to happen. But they did not understand why Jews still felt vulnerable to anti-Semitism. The Jewish world seemed to define itself in terms of resistance to external threats—but it appeared that Israel was one of the more successful and powerful states in the world (not to mention, if recent reports have any accuracy, one of the biggest nuclear powers). Moreover, the Jewish people were succeeding in economic terms to a much greater extent than most other ethnic groups in America. What, other than neurotic guilt or paranoia, would make Jews feel insecure?

Neither the leaders of the Jewish community nor ordinary Jewish parents could supply the answers to these questions. As a result, many children had the feeling that they were dealing with a community of people who had been so deeply scarred by their own history of oppression that they could no longer see their own power.

The truth, I've argued, is that the Jews were and remain in a vulnerable position, but that they can't allow themselves to recognize the real source of that vulnerability—the particular nature of Jewish oppression—because to see that clearly would require the risk of engaging in a struggle to eliminate the oppressive aspects of any society in which they live. Part of the expertise Jews developed as theorists and ideologists derives from the unconscious Jewish desire to avoid looking clearly at our objective situation—because the more that we see it clearly, the more that we realize that there *is* no solution to our own problems without engaging in a struggle to transform the world.

Jewish self-interest, and, ultimately, Jewish survival itself, depends upon tikkun, the Hebrew term for healing, repairing and transforming the world. This kind of transformation is a central goal of Judaism, a central way that Jews understand their mission or sense of "chosenness," and the central meaning of the Jewish God, the force in the universe that makes possible this transformation and healing. Of course, this reading of Torah is only one possible reading, but it has been supported by a significant number of Jewish teachers and prophets throughout Jewish history. The Torah's frequent warnings of what would happen to the Jewish people if they didn't live a life based in Torah could boil down to this: If we do not have a world based on love, compassion, and justice, then you, the Jewish people, will not be safe and secure. It is in your self-interest to create such a world. To the extent that you are *really* the people of Israel, you are the people whose task it is to engage in this struggle.

Not surprisingly, there are not very many Jews today who want the Jewish people to be "the people of Israel" in this sense—because to be Israel in this sense would involve putting in danger our commodious living and our comfortable lifestyles, and put ourselves at real risk. Yet the alternative, to attempt to make accommodations to a world of oppression, has not worked well either, because the Jews end up becoming victims when things get rough in the world.

Because younger Jews of the New Left could not understand the nature of Jewish oppression, and because their largely assimilated parents gave them precious little knowledge of the details of Jewish history, Jewish oppression remained invisible to them, and they failed to struggle against anti-Semitism in the 1960s and 1970s.

Identification with Others Who Were Oppressed

One reason Jews might have been less worried about facing the same risk of being a "target group" in the postwar U.S. is that the role of the "evil Other" had been fulfilled before Jews started arriving in the U.S. in the 1880s.

Blacks had been enslaved for hundreds of years. When freed from slavery, Blacks remained the most oppressed group in America and the group typically focused on as the evil Other. Jews, on the other hand, to the extent that they could shave their beards, straighten their hair, get plastic surgery on their noses, develop "polite" behaviors, and talk softly and moderately, might fit in to the society, not be so noticed, and actually slide through.

Jews were not in the forefront of oppressing Blacks. Though a small number of Jews had been involved in the slave trade throughout history, most slave traders were not Jews and most Jews were not slave traders. Nor were Jews the ones who owned the large corporations that had used Blacks as strikebreakers, setting up an antagonism between them and various European immigrant communities of white workers. Nor were the Jews those who constructed or enforced segregation in the South or who created the economy that underpaid Blacks in the North.

Nevertheless, in the postwar years Jews were increasingly in that part of the economy where they became public faces of the large exploiters and private exploiters on their own. Many of those who eventually became involved in the New Left and other social change movements since the 1960s grew up in families that employed Black domestics, usually on terms that undervalued the work they were giving to the family, and frequently on terms that were not only economically oppressive but also socially demeaning. Other Jewish families who did not employ Black domestics had other kinds of economic relationships that involved inequalities of power. Some owned ghetto property, property that these Jews had themselves once lived in and that they now rented to Blacks at rates that too often felt like a squeeze to the renters, or that they now used to sell goods to Blacks at prices higher than those at suburban stores. (But after all, argued the Jewish shopkeepers, one has to compensate for losses from crime and other risks of doing business in the ghetto.)

Other Jews dealt with Blacks as teachers and social workers, often trying to share the values and the wisdom that had made it possible for the Jews to succeed, but nevertheless placed in situations in which they often had to end up as disciplinarians trying to enforce "acceptable behavior" on a population that was rebellious. Particularly as Blacks began to struggle for civil rights and then for Black liberation, Jewish children were faced with the reality that their own parents, or others in the Jewish community that they had grown up in, seemed to be involved in oppressive or exploitative relationships with Blacks. Without any understanding of the peculiar forms of Jewish oppression, many of these future New Leftists found themselves angered at Jewish behavior and convinced that Jews were more oppressors than oppressed.

Many of these Jewish children drew an important and largely correct lesson from the Holocaust: that one ought to put great energy into the struggle against racism. We can be proud that many young

Jews immediately understood that this lesson meant that Jews ought to be fighting on behalf of the victims of racism—and in America, that meant fighting on behalf of Blacks. But because these same young Jews often did not understand the specific way that Jewish oppression functions, they mistakenly concluded that it was only someone else, and *not* the Jews, who were in danger as potential victims of societal racism.

Angry at their parents and other Jews who participated in the racist realities of American society, many New Leftists could not imagine that their fellow Jews might be both exploiters in some respects and oppressed in other respects, much less that the situation that had put some Jews in the position of being exploiters was itself part of the way Jewish oppression functions.

It was precisely this inability to recognize their own complex role in society that allowed some of these Jews to idealize the oppressed, to feel that one could learn all truths from them. Had they studied their own history they would have learned that oppression breeds distortion as well as nobility, stupidity as well as wisdom. No wonder many of these Jews found themselves disappointed and disillusioned as one after another of the various oppressed groups turned out to be less exemplary and more contradictory than they had expected them to be! Yet even at the moments when this disillusionment set in, few of the Jews who had been active in the New Left actually allowed themselves to consider the possibility that perhaps they had been too hard on their own people, or that perhaps the prejudices of their parents were not really any worse than the misdirected angers and fears of any other oppressed group. It was very difficult for Jews in the New Left to feel any compassion for themselves or for their own people, no matter how much they might preach compassion for others.

Self-Loathing

Young Jews growing up in postwar society may not have encountered the overt threats that faced Jews of earlier generations, but they were not exempt from the intense psychological dynamics that face every oppressed group and lead them to internalize anger in the form of self-loathing. In a world that has conveyed the message to Jews that "there is something so wrong with you that you do not

deserve to exist, so we will either facilitate or at least not interfere with the attempts to systematically exterminate you," it is inevitable that the victims begin to feel terrible about themselves.

In her essay "The Dynamics of Anti-Semitism" (*Tikkun*, Volume 6, Number 2), Cherie Brown shows that Jewish self-loathing is manifested in many different forms by different people: in the ways they do not take care of their bodies; in the way they are critical of fellow Jews for not living up to goyish norms (e.g., because they act "too pushy" or "too assertive"); in the way they find themselves "just not liking Jews" (whether that is American Jews who find themselves sexually attracted only to non-Jews, or Israelis who feel contempt for Holocaust survivors or others with a "Diaspora mentality"); in the way they find it easier to criticize than to support fellow Jews; in the way they criticize specifically those Jews who are taking courageous stands (for fear they will endanger the rest of us); or in a general sense of the inevitability of our individual or collective isolation. It is not uncommon for Jews to praise Jewish humor as a mechanism of survival that allows us to laugh at our own foibles; it is much rarer to see how the humor is also at times a form of internalized aggression toward ourselves, an "acceptable" form for deriding stereotypes that have been imposed upon us by the larger society.

Nowhere has that self-loathing been more acute than in the rash of "humor" and aggression against so-called Jewish American Princesses (JAPs). To be sure, every successful racist stereotype builds on some aspect of reality, and so the JAP stereotype derives from the actual experience of what happens to some strong and creative Jewish women who are excluded from the decision-making apparatus of both the Jewish and the larger economic and political worlds, told to serve their husbands' needs and egos, and told that their fulfillment can only take place in the world of consumption. Yet even to the extent that the stereotype works, it ontologizes a condition of oppression as though it were an outgrowth of some women's choice, and it suggests that something either about their status as Jews or their status as women has caused them to be in this situation, hence making the oppressed appear as the oppressor—in many ways a shorthand for what is the unique dynamic of anti-Semitism. That it is Jewish men and, to a lesser but by no means negligible extent, Jewish women who tell these jokes or who hold these stereotypes is a dramatic demonstration of the degree to which self-loathing permeates Jewish consciousness in the Diaspora.

To demand that their comrades in the New Left learn about the specifics of Jewish oppression would have required that Jewish New Leftists have a degree of self-affirmation that they did not have. And given that they likely would have faced a skeptical response to any demands to take Jewish oppression seriously, in the absence of a clear sense of the value of Jewish identity and the evil of racism against Jews, they would have found it difficult to meet the challenge.

Jewish self-loathing is not confined to Jews who were attracted to the New Left; but neither were they particularly exempt from it. To

he extent that Jews denigrated themselves internally, it was abso-
utely inconceivable that they would be able to raise the issue of Jew-
sh oppression within the context of the New Left.

Anti-Semitism on the Left

Like many of their Jewish assimilationist parents, many Jews
vho became active in the Left felt that the best way to deal with anti-
emitism was to convince themselves that if they showed they were
lot *too* Jewish, and didn't make too much of it, they would not offend
heir non-Jewish colleagues (who, consciously or unconsciously, they
uspected would react with anti-Semitism if Jews *did* make too much
f a fuss about their Jewishness). Largely unconscious of the degree to
vhich they sought to pass, Jews attempted to adopt modes of dress
nd accent that would not allow them to be identified with New York
which was a common code word for "too Jewish"), insisted on how
nuch they detested their Jewish backgrounds and how powerfully
hey could critique Israel, and in other ways attempted to reassure
heir non-Jewish comrades that they would not be imposing a Jewish
genda on the New Left. Nor were they merely fantasizing the exis-
ence of a problem. There is no particular reason to think that non-
ews on the Left had mysteriously transcended the anti-Semitism that
ad been endemic to the West generally and to the history of the Left.

Women and African Americans had both faced massive resis-
ance and powerful, though often unconscious, racism and sexism
vhen they attempted to raise their issues within the Left. Yet in both
ases, the oppressed groups could find clear contemporary evidence
f one kind of oppression: economic exploitation. Jewish oppression
id not take this form.

Not that all Jews have "made it." Although some upper-middle-
lass Jews have been so isolated by class barriers that they have liter-
lly never encountered Jews who are not affluent, the fact is that there
re Jews who are poor, many Jews who are part of the working class,
nd many who are struggling in lower- or middle-income jobs. There
re hundreds of thousands of Jews with working-class jobs or lower-
niddle-class incomes who struggle to survive, often face the crime
nd uncertainty of decaying urban centers, and deeply and justifiably
esent the assumption frequently voiced in liberal circles that all Jews
re prospering. But while not all Jews are affluent, Jews are not eco-

nomically oppressed *as Jews*—that is, their Jewishness is not a primary factor in preventing their economic mobility.

For many Jews in liberal and progressive circles, the fact that Jewish oppression was not economic made it hard for them to imagine presenting an argument about Jewish oppression. Not fully understanding how one could be oppressed if one was not economically oppressed, many of these progressive Jews were in no position to articulate this to their non-Jewish comrades on the Left, who they correctly imagined would be resistant to this kind of concern.

Ironically, though, it was the Jews in the New Left who took the lead in articulating new concepts of cultural and social oppression that transcended the vulgar Marxism that validated only economic deprivation as "real." Betty Friedan, Gloria Steinem, and hosts of other Jewish women were in the forefront of developing a new conception of oppression that was no longer restricted to economic realities, but that took into account the quality of human relationships and the nature of social realities. How large a step was it really from being able to understand that even a relatively wealthy woman might still be a victim of sexism, or that an economically successful gay person might still be a victim of homophobia, to realizing that even an economically successful Jew might still be vulnerable to anti-Semitism? Perhaps unconsciously, the Jews who became the leadership of the New Left, and of the feminist and gay movements that it helped spawn, were themselves groping for a conceptual framework in which to understand Jewish oppression—yet too oppressed themselves in this respect actually to address the issue of Jewish oppression head-on.

It is no surprise, then, that *Tikkun* has become the voice of those who seek to shift the liberal and progressive social-change movements away from what remains a very narrow conception of human beings and human needs. Despite the fact that most people involved with these movements would never think of themselves as committed to vulgar Marxism, they nevertheless tend to see human beings as fundamentally motivated by material needs and the need for freedom from constraint. Hence, the politics of the liberal and progressive world, even of many people in the ecology movement, tends to be a politics of economic entitlements and political rights. When they try to extend this way of thinking to ecological issues, for example, they personify the planet as "mother earth" and then talk about *her survival rights*.

Counter to this, *Tikkun* has argued that while it supports the struggle for economic entitlements and political rights, it believes that there is another and deeper set of human needs—the need to have a life that is embedded in a community of meaning and purpose, that provides an ethical and spiritual foundation for existence and links one to a meaningful past and future. Human beings are fundamentally social and in need of each other, and our struggle for a meaningful life finds expression in family life, communities, and the world of work. Given the actual organization of oppressive class societies, however, this need for meaning gets systematically frustrated—and *the deprivation of meaning* is every bit as pressing as the deprivation of material goods. The success of the Right has been its ability to validate those needs, and to attempt to provide a set of substitute gratifications (e.g. through encouraging us to fantasize that we are all part of some unalienated "we" such as the nation, religious community, or white race) to keep our attention diverted from the way that those needs are not met in daily life. But when these substitute gratifications do not provide the community people are seeking, the Right then poses the possibility that there is some "Other" that is at fault, and this has included gays, Jews, Communists, Arabs, Japanese, and, most prominently in the U.S., Blacks.

The Right has been successful because the Left doesn't even contend on this terrain, but instead cedes the whole set of concerns to the Right. When people on the Left try to raise the issue of the deprivation of meaning, they are dismissed as unduly psychologistic, religious, or flaky. Precisely because the Left is concerned with serious changes to the society, which in any case might be dismissed as visionary and utopian, they feel the need to root their concerns in something "hard" such as economic data or denial of specific rights that constrain action—all things that can be demonstrated empirically. They shy away from these more fundamental human needs, dismiss all discussion about them, and hence misunderstand American politics. *Tikkun* has been trying to change this by launching a campaign for a politics of meaning. This politics of meaning can best help us understand the reality of Jewish oppression. When the deprivation of meaning becomes most acute, it is the Jews who frequently become a target of the pent-up anger and frustration. Conversely, the hidden vulnerability caused by the deprivation of meaning puts Jews into a position in which they feel the need to be like everyone else, hoping that behavioral assimilation will protect them. To do that, however, entails rejecting our own community of meaning and purpose, namely Judaism and Jewish culture and history. This need to deny our particular cultural heritage in order to protect ourselves is another manifestation of the way Jews are oppressed in America and on the Left.

Given all these reasons that Jews did not urge the liberal and progressive social-change movements to pay special attention to anti-Semitism, it is not surprising that the movements have failed to do so. Nevertheless, by failing to do so they "objectively" play an anti-Semitic role, fostering a way of looking at the world that denies the reality of Jewish experience in the past two thousand years, and particularly in the past seventy years.

How Anti-Semitism Functions in Liberal and Progressive Organizations

If we think of the ways in which sexism or homophobia have operated in liberal and progressive organizations, we gain a better understanding of the ways anti-Semitism functions. Just as women did not claim that left-wing men consciously thought all women are inferior, so we do not imagine that people on the Left hate Jews or Jewish traits, or that they couldn't care less about the needs or interests of Jews. Rather, just as women discovered that their needs and interests were systematically ignored or denied, so Jews can find a variety of ways in which Jewish experience and Jewish needs are ignored or denied on the Left. Here I will attempt to discuss a few of the ways this is so.

A. **Issues.** Liberal and progressive organizations systematically ignore Jewish issues around the world. Most liberal and progressive social-change movements gave little or no attention to anti-Semitism in the postwar years, even when it manifested itself in virulent forms, as in acts of violence against Jews during the dictatorship in Argentina, in neo-Nazi violence against Jews in the United States (including a wave of bombings and arsons at synagogues in the last few years), or in the systematic oppression of Jews in the Soviet Union. There is no objective criterion by which these forms of oppression and overt racism can be legitimately ignored. Yet the overwhelming majority of liberal and progressive organizations gave little or no attention to them, nor did the fact of this oppression help in the slightest to weaken the Left consensus that Jews are not one of the oppressed groups of the world. It is inconceivable that similar oppression of women or gays or Blacks would have been similarly ignored.

B. **Leadership.** Because Jews are not considered an oppressed group, Jews are not represented *as Jews* within Left organizations. Although many of these organizations or movements have a disproportionate number of Jews, those Jews who are actually selected for leadership are those who are best able to assure their comrades that they won't raise specifically Jewish issues. On the other hand, anyone who has a strong interest in fighting against Jewish oppression, or in what can be learned from the insights of Jewish culture and history, is seen as ethnocentric or potentially reactionary, and hence to be avoided when organizations or movements are picking potential spokespeople or leaders.

C. **Abandoning History and Ethnicity.** Given the commitment to not seeing Jews as oppressed, Jews are in effect required to abandon their own unique history and ethnic identity and instead identify as "whites" in America. This has the convenient consequence for the Left that it does not have to deal with its own history of oppressing Jews, and that it does not have to understand forms of oppression other than those that have already been officially accepted as legitimate. But in so doing, the Left participates in and encourages Jews to participate in the historical amnesia that characterizes Western capitalist societies, an amnesia that actually works mostly to allow people to accept the contemporary reality as the only possible reality (hence, having a conformist and anti-revolutionary consequence).

D. **Eliminating Jews from the Multicultural Context.** The liberal and progressive forces in this society have correctly insisted that the dominant culture taught in the schools and universities has disproportionately represented white European and American males, and has excluded the rich history and culture of other groups. Though far from winning equality of opportunity for other cultures, the Left has been able to force a debate on this issue, and in some places to convince universities or school systems to take remedial action. Yet those who have fought for a multicultural education never acknowledge Jewish insights and wisdom as one of the traditions that have been systematically excluded. The Talmud, Midrash, responsa literature, Jewish medieval and contemporary philosophers and theologians, and Yiddish and Hebrew novelists, poets, and essayists all have been excluded from the canon in the past and are now excluded from the literature being introduced by multiculturalists.

Just as the Left ignores the history of Jewish oppression, so it ignores the exclusion of Jewish culture (unless it is violently suppressed by ruling elites). Ethnic studies programs rarely include Jewish studies; Jewish contributions are rarely part of multicultural courses; and when teachers are hired to teach these subjects, Jews are lumped with white European males as a group that ought not to be part of the pool from which teachers will be drawn.

E. Forcing Jews to Choose Between a Left and a Jewish Identity. Because the liberal and progressive forces cannot recognize or validate Jewish oppression and the reality of anti-Semitism, they put Jews in the difficult position of having to choose between their Jewishness and their progressive politics. While many Jews have already been turned off by the experiences they have inside a conformist and conservative Jewish community, their identification with the Left gives no basis for reconnecting to that community as potential agents of change. Moreover, to the extent that the Jewish community is seen as just another manifestation of a destructive "whiteness" or of "bourgeois values," the Left gives no validation or support to those who do wish to work to change the values and orientation of the Jewish community. In fact, people who put energy in that direction are given no support on the Left.

Tikkun magazine, started in the 1980s as the voice of liberal and progressive American Jews, has sometimes faced this dilemma. We often are told by various leftists, particularly Jews on the Left, that although they know that *Tikkun* is addressing their own areas of interest and concern, they still don't bother to subscribe or to read it regularly because they see *Tikkun* as a Jewish magazine. It doesn't even occur to them to consider the anti-Semitic or self-hating overtones. (Can you imagine the reaction in liberal or progressive circles if an African American said, "I don't read that magazine because, although it has a very interesting perspective and deals with issues of concern to me, it's an African-American magazine"?) In turn, this leads others who want their writing to be taken more seriously to write in other magazines that are not overtly Jewish. This problem is specific to the Left, and not of other constituencies. *Tikkun* has no problem being taken seriously and read extensively by people in the U.S. Congress or state department, by the media or by intellectual and cultural elites. Its essays have been reprinted in *The Best American Essays,* its fiction has won O'Henry Awards, and its cultural analyses are quoted extensively and sometimes even set the terms of the public debate. Yet people on the Left, particularly Jews on the Left, sometimes dismiss it because it is Jewish! The Right did not have this same problem when *Commentary,* a magazine sponsored by the American Jewish Committee and one that deals with both Jewish and general affairs, became the place in which right-wing ideas were put forward and explored. Jeane Kirkpatrick's famous article distinguishing between authoritarian and totalitarian regimes, which became central to the Right's campaign for escalating military expenditures in the 1980s, was published in *Commentary*— and widely read and debated by right-wing ideologues. Jewishness does not disqualify one on the Right or in the political center of American politics. It is primarily the Left that finds it difficult to take seriously a magazine, a speaker or a writer who articulates an explicit commitment to Judaism or who presents himself or herself within a Jewish framework.

Is it any wonder that Jews often find it difficult to function in this Left—particularly to the degree that Jews have a positive sense of their own identity as Jews? Is it any wonder that it is difficult for Jews to recruit fellow Jews to participate in this Left, unless they already share to some extent the internalized anti-Semitism that predominates among many leftist Jews?

I am *not* contending that all Jews on the Left participate in this internalized anti-Semitism. On the contrary, I am presenting an analysis that is itself the product of the thinking of many Jews who are involved in the liberal and progressive movements, who intend to stay committed to and involved in those movements, and who are nevertheless proudly identified as Jews. Nor am I contending that Jews ought to leave the Left or that Jews who join it are somehow suspect.

But I am claiming that it is easier to function as a Jew on the Left to the degree to which you already reject your Jewishness, and that this weakens the Left, pushes away a potential constituency, and creates a certain set of conflicts that Jews working on the Left think they *ought* not to deal with.

Every person in liberal and progressive organizations must face these issues squarely and rethink her or his relationship to the issue of anti-Semitism. You must ask yourself, have you been avoiding the issue? Are you so annoyed at the policies of the present government of Israel that you've been insensitive to the problem of how easily anti-Semitism can reappear under the guise of legitimate criticism? If you are a Jew in these movements, have you been avoiding the issue perhaps because you have your own scores to settle with the Jewish establishment or with your parents? Just as not only men but also women on the Left came to realize that they had to rethink their relationship to the whole issue of sexism, so not only non-Jews but Jews as well have to rethink their relationship to the whole history and current reality of Jew-hating in the world and Jew-hating on the Left.

7

Israel: Legitimate Criticisms vs. Israel-bashing and Anti-Semitism

What makes the entire issue of criticism of Israel so complicated is that correct criticisms can sometimes be used in an anti-Semitic manner. Nevertheless, not every criticism is necessarily anti-Semitic, and it is certainly unreasonable to say that a state that has been created as a refuge for those who have been subject to oppression is automatically free of criticism. Much depends on how that criticism is offered, how fairly, and in what context.

Legitimate Criticism

Sometimes people in the Jewish media or the Jewish establishment claim that they oppose only illegitimate criticisms of Israel, but in practice it appears as if any serious criticisms of Israeli policies are automatically relegated to the "illegitimate" category. So if we want to rule out illegitimate criticisms, we ought to be able to present some examples of what we think are legitimate criticisms.

Legitimate Criticism #1. Israel should not be ruling over one-and-a-half million Palestinians who wish to have national self-determination. The Israeli government for years refused to acknowledge the very existence of a Palestinian people, and today refuses to acknowledge their rights to national self-determination. Limited autonomy to run municipal services may eventually be granted, but this is a long way from the recognition of legitimate national rights.

Moreover, by attempting to fill up the West Bank with Jewish settlers (whether as part of a professed goal of reclaiming the historic Judea and Samaria or under the rubric of "settlements for Israel's self-defense"), the Israeli government is "creating facts" that may preclude the most obvious solution to the problem: the division of the land into two states for two peoples, each living at peace with the other.

But isn't this just what all the people who are normally accused of anti-Semitism or being self-hating Jews are actually saying? Sometimes. There are ways of making this perfectly fair criticism that can turn it into a statement that reeks of Jew-hating and double standards. Our criticism does not imply that Israel *intended* to do something wrong when it got into this situation, nor that the *blame for the origin of the problem* should be placed on Israel's shoulders. Instead, we focus only on the current reality and why *it* is not acceptable, and suggest what would be acceptable. But many people put forward the criticism in ways that unfairly blame Israel, and this not only invokes double standards and anti-Semitism, it also impedes the ability of many Jews even to hear what *is* legitimate in the criticism of Israeli policy.

These blaming accounts are usually historically biased and inaccurate. Consider the following: Israel's conquest of the West Bank came in response to a 1967 war that was precipitated by the surrounding Arab states. After the Suez Invasion of 1956 (in which Israel, France, and England jointly invaded Egypt in response to President Nasser's nationalization of the Suez Canal and shutting it to Israeli shipping), Israel agreed to withdraw from the Sinai in exchange for the creation of a UN "peace-keeping force" that would stand between Egypt and Israel. But in 1967, Nasser suddenly demanded withdrawal of the force, and within a matter of weeks, the U.N. complied. Nasser began to move his troops into an offensive position facing Israel from the Sinai, complete with radio broadcasts talking about pushing the Jews into the sea. (Is it any wonder that today many Israelis look with deep cynicism on promises of protection from "an international force" that is supposed to guarantee the security of the border between two warring states, when they remember so well this act of betrayal by the United Nations?) A mere twenty-two years after the Holocaust, another dictator was talking about wiping out the Jewish people and the world seemed to be sitting by idly once again!

No one knows for sure what Egypt or Syria would have done, but their actions and public statements would have given anyone reasonable grounds for great fear. Before Egypt or Syria could attack, Israel launched the Six Day War, devastating the Egyptian army and also capturing the Golan Heights in Syria, from which Syrians had been bombing Israeli kibbutzim in the valley below.

Israel appealed to King Hussein of Jordan *not* to enter the war, but to Israel's dismay the Jordanians joined with Egypt and Syria, launching attacks from its positions in the West Bank and East Jerusalem. In the ensuing struggle, Israel conquered the divided city of Jerusalem and the West Bank.

Soon thereafter, there were calls for an independent Palestinian state. But Israelis countered with a legitimate response: Why had there been no call for an independent Palestinian state during the years when an Arab country occupied the West Bank? Didn't this show that the newfound support for Palestinian nationalism was nothing but a new vehicle in the ongoing struggle of the Arab states to eliminate Israel completely?

Israel may have been correct about the intentions of at least some of those who now supported Palestinian self-determination. And they certainly were not reassured by the charter of the Palestinian Liberation Organization, which explicitly called for the elimination of the State of Israel. For many years the PLO called for the creation of a Palestinian state as the *first stage* in a two stage struggle; the second stage would be the "total liberation of Palestine" (by which it meant the elimination of Israel). Palestinian leaders talked of shipping Jews back to their "country of origin," thereby refusing to acknowledge the long, historical connection of the Jewish people to the Land of Israel. None of this reassured Israel that the Palestinians or surrounding states were ready to live in peace. Most Israelis feared a Palestinian state and rejected the claims of the Palestinians for national self-determination.

Meanwhile, what had been intended as a temporary occupation became a permanent fact of life, one that most Israelis had not sought, but which a few—the religious messianists of the right-wing Gush Emunim—believed to represent the will of God and the historic destiny of the Jewish people to return to the full Land of Israel as described in the Bible.

The point of this historical picture is that it is totally unfair to allow the Occupation to be described, as it sometimes is by various groups on the Left, as "Israeli expansionism," "Israeli imperialism," "Israeli colonialism," or the like. Israel did not occupy the territories out of some inner drive for expansion or to satisfy religious or Zionist aspirations, but rather in response to a real military threat. It is inconceivable, for instance, to imagine the United States, Russia, France, or any other state in similar circumstances *not* taking military action to protect itself. Any government in a democratic society that had *not* acted decisively would soon have been replaced.

Israelis continue to indicate in various public opinion polls that if they believed the Palestinians and surrounding Arab states would live in peace with Israel, abandon all claims to the land within the pre-1967 boundaries of Israel, and abandon all acts of terrorism or political agitation and instead seek a "warm peace," they then would be willing to exchange land for peace. But Israelis do not believe that Palestinians really want this kind of warm peace.

Israelis are unwilling to believe Palestinians or other Arabs who talk about peace, because the Israelis have been so brutalized by the past history of anti-Semitism that it is hard for them to believe any non-Jew talking about treating the Jews right. Partly, their skepticism is based on the fact that Palestinian and Arab opposition has been so violent and so clear in its determination to destroy Israel that current talk about peace seems to be a tactical switch designed to win world public opinion. Their skepticism is also based on the continuing volume of anti-Semitic rhetoric that has been integrated into the media and educational systems of the Arab world and that finds expression in the absolutely uncompromising position of Islamic fundamentalists who reject the notion of a Jewish state in *any* part of the Middle East. Their skepticism is reinforced by the fact that some Palestinian groups continue to engage in acts of terror against Israeli civilians.

Certainly there are some whose skepticism is based on a total unwillingness ever to consider giving up any part of the Land of Israel. But there are many Israelis—the majority according to most polls—who would consider exchanging land for peace.

We at *Tikkun* question this skepticism. Many of us feel that Israel ought to be taking major steps toward peace now. Israel has the most powerful army in the region; it would not be militarily threatened by a Palestinian state if that state were demilitarized and its demilitarization were carefully supervised and unambiguously enforced. We have been critical of every Israeli government, whether of Likud, Labor, or "National Unity," that does not take decisive steps toward peace. Most importantly, we believe the government should accept, in principle, the right of the Palestinians to national self-determination in a state of their own, provided that state was fully demilitarized and provided that state renounced, in the name of the Palestinian people, all claims to land in the pre-1967 borders of the state of Israel.

While we agree that the Occupation is unjust, we disagree that it can be understood in terms such as "colonialist" or "imperialist."

The Occupation leads Israel to pursue an unjust policy, oppressive to the Palestinians and ultimately self-destructive to Israel and the Jewish people, primarily because Israelis are scared about their own survival. We believe that a Palestinian state, if demilitarized, would not constitute a military threat, and that continuation of the Occupation in any form, even in the form of the "limited autonomy" envisioned by Camp David and advocated by the Rabin wing of the Israeli Labor party, would actually be *more* of a threat to Israel's longterm survival and to its political support around the world. We believe that Israelis who resist the notion of an independent demilitarized Palestinian state are deeply mistaken. But we understand this resistance as fear. If we conclude that this fear is destructive, that Israelis are paranoid, and that they really could live in peace with Palestinians, then our task and the world's task is to cure this paranoia. But remember this:

A world that has for thousands of years oppressed the Jewish people is in no position to talk cavalierly about paranoia without constantly acknowledging its role in generating the paranoia.

The way to cure Israeli fears is not to denounce them as irrational, but to acknowledge and address the rational component in the fear, while simultaneously behaving in ways that slowly reassure the Jewish people that its pain and oppression have been understood and will not be repeated.

The way that most people in liberal and progressive movements act is just the opposite. The Left's ignorance of the history presented in this book, and its unwillingness to acknowledge and struggle against the long history of anti-Semitism on the Left, reinforces paranoia and ultimately gives credibility and strength to right-wing forces in the Jewish world.

Legitimate Criticism #2. While the Occupation continues, Israel ought to recognize the human rights of the Palestinian people and treat them in accord with the internationally recognized standards of human rights that we expect of all civilized countries. Israel must stop the torture of detainees, must stop the practice of incarcerating people without charges and without trials for six-month, renewable "administrative detentions," must allow unimpeded visitation by families of the incarcerated, must stop the process of blowing up family homes for the crimes of one family member, must stop the deportation of people charged with a crime, and must stop the expropriation of Arab lands by Israeli settlers.

These are all legitimate demands and should be supported. But it matters a great deal *how* these demands are made—whether, for example, they are made in ways that single out Israel, or are placed in the context of demands on surrounding Arab states for an end to their considerably more serious human-rights violations. In his essay "Talking About Torture in Israel" (*Tikkun,* Volume 6, Number 6), Stanley Cohen, professor of criminology at Hebrew University, details the facts of Israeli torture and discusses the issue with the complexity and attention to nuance that seem appropriate and fair-minded. Yet it would have been wrong for *Tikkun* to focus on this torture if we had not similarly focused throughout the years on torture and human-rights violations in other countries, including Syria, Iraq, and Egypt, as well as countries like Cuba and Nicaragua under the Sandinistas.

Legitimate Criticism #3. Israel should stop discriminating against its own Arab citizens in housing, employment, education, and allocation of funds to municipalities, and Israeli citizens should confront and stop their racist attitudes toward Palestinians and Arabs.

People living in Western societies should make this criticism with appropriate modesty and full acknowledgment of the racist practices that tend to characterize most of the advanced industrial societies.

Legitimate Criticism #4. Israel should not impose religion on its own citizens. While Israel has a legitimate right to be a Jewish state in the same sense that Italy or France have the right to be Italian or French states (and thereby give a privileged attention to the literature of the Italian or French people over that of various Italian or French minority groups), and to privilege Jewish holidays in the same way that the U.S. privileges Christian and American holidays, it ought *not* to use the power of the state to force religion down anyone's throat. Israel ought to allow secular marriage and divorce, and ought to avoid giving religious students or religious people special dispensations from national service or special access to financial support.

Moreover, there is an additional part of the criticism that is legitimate if made by those committed to Judaism: *Any* sanction of religion by the state is likely to work against the best interests of Judaism. Those of us who want to see Judaism survive in Israel believe it can do so only if it renounces all association with state power. Even so, it will take decades to overcome the negative associations that Judaism has acquired in the minds of most Israelis, because religious parties have used state power to coerce religious practice and because they have cynically manipulated the proportional representation system of the Knesset to achieve funding of their schools and projects.

On the other hand, this criticism can also be made in illegitimate ways. Israel has a right to set up a Jewish society, privileging Jewish culture, history, literature, and religion. Those who are agitated about Israel giving special privileges to Jewish culture, trying thereby to create a Jewish state, ought to be careful that they are similarly agitated when the Catholic majority of Mexico or the Islamic majority in Algeria or the Hindu majority in India trying to privilege their religion in their public cultural life.

Legitimate Criticism #5. Israel privileges European experience, culture, and lifestyle over that of the Middle East. The current Ashkenazi elite that governs the major Israeli parties often manifests contempt for the culture and historical background of the Israeli majority who came to Israel from Morocco, Tunisia, Algeria, Egypt, Syria, Yemen, Iraq, Iran, Turkey, and other non-Western countries. These Sephardim and Mizrachim are subjected to an intensive campaign to "educate" them to Western values and Western ways.

There's an important truth in this criticism and it behooves the Israeli peace movement to take it seriously. The Labor party, the most prominent pro-peace party in Israeli politics, was in power when most of these Middle Eastern Jews arrived in Israel in the 1950s and 1960s; it was the Labor party that presided over the attempts to modernize those immigrants and introduce them to a supposedly higher culture. As doves in the Sephardi and Mizrachi worlds have shown their Ashkenazi colleagues in the peace movement, if peace is going to come to Israel, these psychic wounds must be healed, and the Left must repudiate its paternalism toward Middle Eastern Jews.

On the other hand, it is a mistake to essentialize or idealize non-Western cultures. As I've argued already, oppression does not necessarily generate the best traits in the oppressed, and that goes for Ashkenazim as well as Sephardim. Anyone who has seen the level of chauvinism and oppression of women in some sectors of the Middle Eastern world, or who has witnessed the readiness of some Middle Eastern Jews to engage in violence to resolve disputes (particularly with the Palestinians), knows that these issues are complex. Some of the values that the Labor party Ashkenazim were trying to inculcate (e.g., respect for women or restraint in the use of violence) may have had their roots in socialist values that were derived from a Torah tradition that came out of the Near East and not out of the West. Violence, sexual abuse, and oppression of women are also real problems among Ashkenzim, and Sephardim are right to resent a moral or cultural elitism and paternalism that sometimes enters these discussions. But many Mizrachim find the attempt to idealize Sephardim and Mizrachim just as paternalistic as the attempt to systematically denigrate them.

While the details of these criticisms may change in the years ahead, and while now or in the future there may be other areas in which it is legitimate to criticize Israel, we've listed these areas as examples of the fact that one *can* engage in legitimate and balanced criticism of the State of Israel without *necessarily* being anti-Semitic. **The problem is that any of these criticisms can be made in anti-Semitic ways.** To understand how legitimate criticism or truth-saying can be racist, let's switch to a more familiar context, that of American racism towards Blacks.

Imagine that a white male candidate decides to run for President of the U.S. and puts forth as part of his platform the notion that Americans must give special attention to fighting what he calls "Black crime and other pathologies in the underclass in contemporary America." In television ads and in public speeches, he dedicates a quarter of his time to excoriating "Black crime" and enumerates over and over again a few aspects of life in African American communities—the assaults of Blacks on other Blacks and also whites, the higher percentage of Blacks arrested for rape or sexual assault than other specific ethnic groups that the candidate details, the higher percentage of Blacks who are arrested for murder. "Black murderers," the candidate charges, "must be taught a lesson—they can no longer get away with these crimes." When asked about crimes in the white population, he readily admits that there is a problem, and acknowledges that he will also need to deal with this. But in the focus of his campaign, in his television ads, speeches, and other public pronouncements, the problems and pathologies in the Black world are disproportionately the focus of his campaign energy and expenditure of resources.

When confronted with charges of racism, the candidate argues that this is not his main issue, that he only spends a quarter of his time on it, and that he is more concerned with lowering taxes, stopping the drug trade, getting jobs for all Americans, and solving environmental problems. Most importantly, he argues, the facts that he is citing are irrefutably true—they've been drawn from data in the public domain that anyone can verify. If people are responding to this issue, he maintains, it is because they themselves know the truth about this issue—after all, for years they've seen incidents of Black crime dramatized on television news as well as in crime shows.

Most liberals and progressives would quickly recognize that this candidate was engaging in overtly racist activity. But what makes it racist? Here are some important features:

1. **A racist selection of the facts becomes a double standard.** Even if it were true that a higher percentage of Blacks had engaged in violent crimes, the decision to focus only on Black crime and not on white crime, to select one group, is racist. To tell the whole story, to see it in context, one would need to talk about the crimes of all people in society. One might start, for example, by talking about the culture of criminality generated by high officials who, in both the Watergate and later the Iran/contra scandals, were shown to violate laws consciously and systematically. The scandal surrounding the illegal activities of the BCCI is only the latest round of criminality in the highest circles of finance and industry. It is well known that the amount of crime exposed among whites would be far higher

if law enforcement officials dedicated more of their energies to these crimes than to ensuring their own version of law and order in poor neighborhoods.

2. **The history and contemporary context of the facts are ignored.** One cannot understand street crime in the African American community without understanding the history of violence against Blacks that has been part of the historical legacy of American society, starting with hundreds of years of violent enslavement and brutality, and continuing with violent repression in the years after emancipation. One of the tragedies of oppression is that those who have been brutalized have a tendency to pass on to others what has been done to them. This is *not* a law of nature, but a strong psychological tendency that can be overcome.[1] The Torah is clear that this could be changed: It urged the Jewish slaves to be sure to remember that when they came into their land they should not do to others what had been done to them. But making this change is difficult, and it needs very supportive conditions. The contemporary realities of American life certainly do not provide these conditions. On the contrary, the distribution of wealth and power is significantly stacked against Blacks, and the society has a long history of discrimination in employment and education that has led to a significantly higher incidence of unemployment and poverty among Blacks than other sectors of the population. To talk of Black crime outside of this context is a racist distortion.

3. **Focusing on the "crimes" of the sector of the population that has for long been the group most oppressed and most subject to racism is necessarily going to have racist consequences, and increase racism within the population.** An objective look at such crime may be possible, but a special focus on it in the political arena will always be racist until many years after the society has finally managed to stamp out all vestiges of racism. One of the consequences of a long history of racism is that even those who think they are free of racism have internalized racist ideas and attitudes that crop up unconsciously.

For all these reasons, most liberals and progressives would have

---

[1] And just as Blacks are *not* the only victims of past brutalization, so they are also *not* the only or chief perpetrators of violence in this society. As I've argued, it is for racist reasons that the violence in *their* community gets special media attention.

Israeli treatment of the Palestinians violates Jewish ethics and undermines Israel's image as a society committed to democratic and human-rights values. Yet some of the ways that criticism has been levelled from the Left have been unfair and have used double standards—judging Israel more harshly than societies with far worse human rights abuses.

little difficulty noticing that a political candidate or movement that gave special focus to the evils or crimes of the Black community was essentially racist and fostering racism. The same criteria apply to the way the Left should deal with criticism of Israel. That is, legitimate criticisms of Israel can be made in an anti-Semitic way if they fall roughly into the categories that made the attack on "Black crime" racist. For example:

1. **A progressive group that gives disproportionate time and energy to criticizing what is wrong with Israel is prima facie engaged in anti-Semitic activity.** What counts as "disproportionate?" This, too, depends on context. On the one hand, it seems reasonable for people to give more attention to problems that are closer to home than problems that are further away, or problems in which one's own country is directly or indirectly implicated. So, by this criterion

it makes sense that American leftists would give special attention to countries that the U.S. has helped support militarily or economically. On the other hand, as people who are part of a liberal or progressive tradition in the world, leftists also have to give special attention to the problems of the countries that the Left has had some special relationship to, either because leftist ideals were used to create them, or because other states that espoused leftist ideals have been traditional allies or supporters.

In this regard, for example, leftists have a special responsibility for denouncing crimes in countries such as China, Cuba, Nicaragua (under the Sandinistas), and even in the countries of Eastern Europe that now yearn for capitalism; but also in states like Russian-armed Syria and Iraq, or states that have a long history of articulating anti-imperialist rhetoric, such as India, Pakistan, Iran, Indonesia, Vietnam, or North Korea.

If one studies the newspapers, public speeches, and demonstrations of various leftist groups and finds that, relative to the actual amount of torture, violation of human rights, violation of international law, and dispossession of national minorities, the Left has been giving consistent and proportionate criticism, then the criticisms of Israel cannot legitimately be called Israel-bashing or anti-Semitic. But in fact, in the experience of most who have observed Left groups functioning in the U.S. and other Western countries, Israel has received a disproportionate amount of attention and criticism. This is anti-Semitic Israel-bashing.

2. When listening to criticisms of Israel, it is important to hear the degree to which these criticisms are put within the historical context of oppression of the Jews by Christian and Islamic societies for the past many centuries, and more recently by the Holocaust. Just as it is racist not to raise the historical context in discussing "Black crime," so it is anti-Semitic Israel-bashing when this context is not repeatedly brought into the discussion. Similarly, criticisms of Israel that do not educate people at the same time to the history of Arab rejectionism, and to the explicit anti-Semitism that has existed and continues to exist in the Islamic world and in Arab cultures become anti-Semitic Israel-bashing.

3. When groups on the Left expect and demand that Israel adhere to a higher standard of behavior than they expect from other

regimes in the area, they are usually involved in anti-Semitic Israel-bashing. Imagine, for example, if some man were to attack a woman for showing an openness to or interest in multiple sexual liasons, and held that this was outrageous because while he knew that men typically engage in the same behavior, he expects something higher or better from women. Would you have trouble deciphering the sexism in this double standard? The Jewish people and the State of Israel do *not* ask the world to judge them by a higher criterion—and the world has *no* right to do so. Imposing a higher standard is the flip side of degradation: The Jews cannot be treated as normal; they are either seen as better or worse than others, but not just as regular human beings with all the normal weaknesses, distortions, pains and also all the normal pleasures, strengths, and beauty.

We shall deal below with the special case of Jews using a double-standard.

Even when all these other considerations have been scrupulously addressed, there remains the general problem of whether it is possible, given the long history and continuing legacy of anti-Semitism, for any criticism to be offered in Western or Islamic countries that does not play into a pre-existing history of racist prejudice, and thus to have anti-Semitic consequences. This cannot be a decisive consideration that prevents all criticism, but it must be a factor that shapes *how* the criticisms are offered.

Those who offer criticisms of a group that has been the target of racism for long periods in history must carefully and systematically show that they are aware of the dangers of playing into the history of racism, that they are consciously aware of how that racism functions, and that they are taking systematic steps in all of their statements and writings simultaneously to confront and disavow that racism or anti-Semitism even as they make their specific and limited criticisms.

These are tough criteria, and they are meant to be. They should not, however, stop any of us from decrying the situation faced by the Palestinian people, identifying with their pain, and demanding that Israel stop the current policies that oppress the Palestinians. On the contrary: Once we are clear about what anti-Semitism is and how to delineate it carefully, we can also sympathize with the oppression of other groups, and identify powerfully with their pain and their struggle for national liberation.

Illegitimate Criticism

Now let's turn to some classic unfair and illegitimate criticisms of Israel.

1. Israel's occupation of the West Bank is racist or a variation of apartheid. In the apartheid system, Blacks were denied the right to equal representation and were prevented legally from living in certain places or using certain public resources or facilities. The determining factor was race, and so the system was racist.

But in Israel, those Palestinians who live within the pre-1967 border of Israel are *not* legally restricted. They have full participation in the electoral system, and while some choose to vote for specifically anti-Zionist parties (and those parties are represented in the Israeli Knesset), others vote for pro-Zionist parties, and as a result the parties on the Left tend to compete for the Palestinian vote. Palestinians swim at the same beaches, attend the same universities, and use the same buses as Israelis. This is not a system of apartheid. Those who do *not* have the vote and do *not* have equal rights are those Palestinians who live in the Occupied Territories. While we oppose the Occupation and support the creation of a demilitarized Palestinian state, we dispute any claim that Israel is an apartheid system or fundamentally racist.

On the other hand, there is plenty of racism among Israelis, just as there is racism among virtually every people. Moreover, there *is* discrimination in Israel against Palestinians who live within the pre-1967 borders of Israel, roughly akin to the kind of discrimination against African Americans that existed in the North of the U.S. previous to the civil-rights movement, and that still exists in many parts of the U.S. today. That discrimination and those racist attitudes ought to be fought—but not confused with a system of apartheid or state-sanctioned racism.

2. Israel has no right to exist because it was set up at the expense of another people. Israel has as much right to exist as any state in the world. True, the creation of Israel resulted in the dispossession of many Palestinians, though that was in part the fault of the Palestinians who refused the 1947 partition agreement. But if the right of a state to exist is based on whether it was set up at the expense of another people, there would hardly be a single state remaining in the world. Those who raise the question of the *right* of Israel to exist are fundamentally anti-Semitic, according to the criteria articulated above, because they do not simultaneously and consistently challenge the right of Iraq to exist (and the consequent oppression of the Kurds), the right of the United States to exist (with its consequent oppression of native peoples), the right of India to exist (with its consequent oppression of Muslims), or the right of Communist China to exist (with its consequent oppression of many minority communities).

3. **Israel is currently the world's worst human-rights abuser.** Israel has systematically engaged in torture and abuse of human rights. But its level of abuse does not approach those in countries such as Iraq, Iran, India, China, Syria, or many countries in Africa. No one who has read through human-rights reports of various monitoring organizations could possibly argue that Israel is the worst. Those who say it is, or who act in ways that convey the message that it is, are promoting anti-Semitism.

Needless to say, Israel should be pressured to change its human-rights picture. It would be perfectly reasonable to argue for a legal ban on aid—government or individual—to any country that was known to engage in systematic violations of human rights. If this ban were executed equitably, it might pressure the Israeli government.

Do Jews Have the Right to Apply a Double Standard to Israel?

My answer to the question posed here is: Some Jews do and some Jews don't. Let me explain.

Jews have a right to a double standard toward Jews (that is, judging Jews by a higher standard than one judges others) if and only if one has a special loving relationship to Judaism and the Jewish people. Many Jews have internalized so much of the larger society's antagonism towards Judaism and Jews that they don't have that special relationship, and hence they have no right to use a double standard.

A double standard is prima facie wrong. Only when one has established a special relationship with an individual or community, and shown a loving and caring relationship, can one claim the right to expect reciprocity and can ask for special standards. For example, one does have a right to give special criticism to those with whom one is in a loving relationship, because the criticism is itself a manifestation of that caring and love. Not to expect a better form of behavior than that which is prevalent in a world dominated by immorality would be a sign of disrespect. But that expectation is appropriate only when one already has an ongoing loving relationship to those with whom one engages in this double-standard criticism.

There's another basis for a double standard. Judaism requires a high level of moral conduct from the Jewish people as a "vanguard" people whose job is to witness God's presence in the world. Those who are strongly committed to Judaism, and who practice it regularly in their lives (and here we are neutral regarding the particular variant of Judaism one practices), have a right to employ high moral standards in relationship to the Jewish people, and would in fact be violating the Torah if they failed to so.

When a religious Jew, or a person whose life is deeply attached and committed to the Jewish people and its history, culture, and contemporary well-being, engages in criticisms that use a higher standard for judging Israel, that criticism is appropriate and not anti-Semitic.

However, there are many Jews who do not fit these two categories. All too often, we find Jews on the Left who have long ago abandoned a strong attachment either to the Jewish people or to Judaism. I don't blame people who have developed in this direction—in fact, although I disagree with the route they have chosen, after hearing their stories I often find myself respecting some of the people who have made this choice. If I myself had not been exposed to the deep intellectual, spiritual, and moral resources of the prophetic tradition within Judaism, I can easily imagine that I might have been so turned off by my experience of the conservatism, anti-intellectualism, intolerance, materialism, and spiritual emptiness of many that I have met in the organized Jewish community that I would not have remained connected to Jewish practice or to Jewish commitment. If the Jewish world has turned off its own children to Judaism, it has only itself to blame—and should not blame those who were simply never shown the richness and depth of Judaism.

But once those ties no longer exist, so too the right to a double standard disappears. It is not sufficient to say, "I'm Jewish, therefore I have the right to employ a double standard." Being born Jewish or educated about Judaism is not a lifetime warranty to employ a double standard to Jews or Israel. And yet, this is precisely what one often finds on the Left: Jews who provide the ideological and political leadership for an assault on Israel or on the Jewish people. Not that these Jews have *no* right to criticize Israel; they have the *same* right to criticize as non-Jews, with the same standards of constraint and fairness that should exist for non-Jews. But their criticisms *may* be anti-Semitic, if they violate the criteria described above. How can a Jew be anti-Semitic? To answer this question, we need to turn to the phenomenon of the self-hating Jew.

Self-hating Jews

We are very reluctant to use this label loosely, because many of us involved with *Tikkun,* the Committee for Judaism and Social Justice, or the various peace and social-justice movements in the Jewish world, have been labeled "self-hating" merely because we criticize Israel. This misuse of the term is so widespread that for years I refused even to imagine that there really were self-hating Jews. Yet in my twenty-five years of involvement in liberal and progressive social-change organizations, I've often faced "self-hating" Jews, and finally have to acknowledge not only that there are self-hating Jews, but that they are prevalent in some sectors of the Left.

It is easy to see how this could be true when we consider, as an analogue, the phenomenon of self-hating women. In the early days of the second wave of feminism, in the late 1960s and early 1970s, it was not unusual to encounter women who reacted strongly to emerging feminism by saying openly, for example, "I really don't *like* women that much—I really like men much better," or "women are interested only in trivial things, while men are interested in the things that really matter," or "sexism has really never affected my life—I'm too strong and too together to let any man lay a sexist trip on me." "Men don't dare to, so I don't really encounter problems with sexism." Or even, "Women's issues are trivial and shouldn't be allowed to interfere with the more important struggle for civil rights for Blacks or the struggle against American imperialism." It is not hard to recognize that some women have deeply internalized the sexist mentality of this society, even though we are still in the early stages of uncovering all the complicated layers of how these patriarchal attitudes have infused our emotional and intellectual being.

Similarly, it should be no surprise that many African Americans have internalized deep negative feelings about their blackness, and it is precisely this kind of internalization of shame and self-directed anger that is one of the inevitable consequences of living within a racist society.

So why should it be a surprise that many Jews have internalized anti-Semitism, or that some do everything they can to reassure themselves and others around them that they are not "too" Jewish? One of the classic ways they act out this internalized self-hatred is to engage in ferocious criticism of Israel, use double standards, and then justify the double standard because, after all, they too are Jewish.

Only those who have a strong loving connection to the Jewish people or to Judaism have a right to use their Jewishness as a justification for a double standard. If people are in doubt about where they stand, let them ask themselves the following questions: What have I done in the past year to show that I am lovingly committed to Judaism or to the Jewish people, apart from engaging in acts of criticism of Israel or of the Jews? Have I attended religious services, gone to a lecture about Jewish history or culture, been involved in Jewish music, art, or literature, or otherwise shown that I feel a deep attachment to my Jewishness in some positive and affirming way? Have I been engaged in confronting and combatting anti-Semitism at work or in the communities within which I do political organizing? Have I given money to support worthwhile Jewish causes (e.g. the New Israel Fund, Tikkun, charities that fund the Jewish sick or elderly, charitable causes in Israel, the Committee for Judaism and Social Justice, or a local synagogue or Jewish cultural project)? Have I been engaged in some organization or cause that specifically champions Jewish interests and concerns, and not just in those parts of the organization concerned with changing Israeli policy? Have I been engaged in Jewish study, learning about history, culture, or religion, or perhaps have I been seeking to build a spiritual life around my Jewishness? Of course, there is no specific amount of activity that is "the right amount," but many of the people most active in unfairly criticizing Israel by using double standards often have to answer "no" to most of these questions (if they answer them honestly).

If your Jewishness over the past several years has consisted solely in saying what is wrong with Israel or the Jews, then that Jewishness is not a warrant to use a double standard, and you have to use the same standards as non-Jews. But if you *do* use a double standard, even though you can't honestly say that you've been involved in positively affirming your Jewishness, chances are that you are legitimately considered a self-hating Jew. That is, whatever your "rational arguments" for your anger at Israel or at the Jews, there is a strong likelihood that your criticisms are tainted by some internalization of societal anti-Semitism, refracted through your anger at your parents or at others you met when you were growing up, which is now being unfairly transferred onto Israel or the Jewish people as a whole. Just as we would not allow someone who had had several bad experiences with Blacks to now make anti-Black generalizations, or to engage in the kind of blaming of Blacks that we identified as racist above, so we would not allow someone who had had bad experiences growing up in the Jewish world to draw sweeping anti-Jewish or anti-Israel conclusions, and those who did would rightly be called self-hating Jews.[1]

Self-Hating Israeli Jews

Perhaps the strangest kind of self-hating Jews are Israelis who not only repudiate Judaism, but also the entire history and culture of Jews in the Diaspora. Some will even strongly assert that they really aren't Jewish, they are only Israelis, and can't figure out why Diaspora Jews think they have any special right to criticize Israel or any special claim on Israel.

Apart from the obvious disingenuousness of this position (since their government keeps appealing to world Jewry for financial help

---

[1] While I've argued that the Left hassles self-affirming Jews more than the Right, the Left certainly doesn't have a monopoly on self-hating Jews. Many of the biggest assimilationists are those who are attracted to the political Right. These Jews try to show the American ruling class that Jews are really "safe," that they share all the same commitments to capitalism and to competitive and patriarchal values as everyone else, and that they can be just as racist, sexist, or pro-imperialist as anyone. They do their best to adopt the literary standards and cultural norms of the most conservative or most centrist sectors of the society, sure that from there they will be unimpeachable. They can even claim their Jewishness once they are certain that no one will be offended.

What's so bad about being an assimilator? There are three points to remember. First, people are often assimilating to an oppressive society whose only superiority over Jewish society is that it is the victorious and dominant Western society. Assimilators are (sometimes unintentionally) validating this system of oppression when they choose it. Second, people are leaving a society that has been oppressed, in part, because it is understood to be threatening to various systems of oppression. In leaving that society, the assimilator abandons those whose vulnerability has been earned, in part, because of what is good about them, not what is bad. Third, it's very hard to say that anyone can *choose* to assimilate, given the power imbalances involved. This choice is so overdetermined by the sustained attack on Jewish culture and identity that it cannot really be seen as a free choice, but rather is typically, at least in part, the expression of the degree to which the dominant culture has colonized the minds of the oppressed. Once anti-Semitism disappears as an actual force in culture and politics, assimilation will be a possible free choice—but we have yet to reach that point.

and political assistance), it reflects a repudiation of Jewishness that can be understood only in terms of the internalization of anti-Semitic attitudes and norms. Israeli desire to be "a nation like all other nations" without any specialness or special obligations is itself a product of the bitter history of oppression that forms their psyches. No such desire can be seen as uncontaminated—it is one of the predictable choices that one may make to escape a history of pain and suffering. We can understand how galling it is for Israelis to hear others demand of them a higher level of morality than is demanded of others, and to respond by saying, "Just treat me like everyone else. I don't want to be asked to be better." But to the extent that they see "everyone else" as acting immorally and oppressively, the desire to be like everyone else cannot be a desire put forward by anyone who is psychologically whole or integrated. This is a response of the oppressed, a cry of pain from those whose moral sensibilities have been dulled by centuries of oppression; hence it testifies to a continuity with the Jewish past whose legacy of pain still shapes the sensibilities of many Israelis. It's easy to sympathize with the pain that leads people to think they can magically remove themselves from the history that shaped the psyches of their parents and grandparents—but this needs to be treated as a symptom, not as a serious intellectual position.

This symptom emerges in many forms of Israeli posturing: their insistence that they are "independent" and don't really need anyone—ignoring the world's economic and political realities in ways that make *everyone* much more interdependent; their insistence on their individual or collective strength; their desperate attempts to show that their universities are as good as Harvard, Yale, Columbia, or UC Berkeley—without allowing themselves to imagine how much *those* schools are themselves ideological bastions whose "superiority" to lesser institutions has more to do with the role they play in training ruling elites than in the content of the ideas they produce; their attempts to make people acknowledge how impossible it is for outsiders to understand Israeli culture. All of these are indications of an overwhelming and pervasive sense of inferiority and insecurity that touches every aspect of Israeli society and culture. It is this pathological insecurity which drives many Israelis to frantically insist that they really are *not* Jewish, have nothing in common with Diaspora Jews, and have no ties to Jewish history or memory.

Those Israelis who loudly proclaim their freedom from Diaspora

Jewry or a Diaspora mentality are in fact those most deeply tied to it, shaped by it, and doing their best to struggle against the legacy of their own internalized oppression. Such self-hating Jews are a sad reminder of the heavy psychic costs linked to our long history of oppression.

> The appropriate way to deal with this problem, however, is *not* to dismiss it or to hate the self-haters. Self-haters are victims.
>
> Very few people can live in a world that deprecates them without absorbing some of the negative attitudes of the larger culture. Most oppressed people feel some degree of self-hatred.
>
> The appropriate attitude toward them is not disdain, but compassion. Just as we ought to have compassion for African Americans who do not like their blackness or try to disassociate from it and act as "white" as possible, or women who try to pretend they have nothing in common with other women, so we also need compassion for Jews who desperately seek, within whatever context they function, to show others that they are not "too" Jewish.

If the Left is one of the arenas in which a subset of these oppressed people act out their self-hatred, then it's the task of others in the Left gently but firmly to interrupt this behavior and show them it is not the way to achieve popularity or acceptance. Everyone knows to do this when an antifeminist woman or a self-hating Black shows up in Left circles. But they don't know to do this when it comes to self-hating Jews on the Left; the Left itself has too many unresolved feelings of anti-Semitism to recognize the self-hating behavior of some of the Jews among its ranks.

8

How Can Progressives Fight
Anti-Semitism on the Left?

If we were not ourselves supporters of the liberal and progressive social-change movements, we would not be so upset about anti-Semitism on the Left. Unfortunately, these movements are not the most powerful force in American society; there is little chance of leftist policies being implemented at every level of society. From our perspective, this is a shame. If the women's movement, ecological movement, civil-rights movement, disarmament movement, gay- and lesbian-rights movement, and other progressive forces could have their programs adopted and implemented, American society would be in better shape.

Part of the reason for the relative isolation of liberal and progressive forces has to do with their inability to create a politics that manifests compassion and concern for ordinary Americans. As becomes evident in the *Tikkun Anthology* and in the ongoing discussions of American political life that take place in *Tikkun* magazine, many Americans perceive the Left as hostile to their real cares and concerns. Most people feel disapproved of and looked down upon by the Left.

In my own work on the Left, I've come to believe that the problem of left-wing elitism is actually a manifestation of a self-blame on the Left that corresponds to the self-blame in the larger society. Most people have come to believe that society's conception of itself as a meritocracy, a society in which you can make it if you try and if you deserve to succeed, is accurate. In fact, the society is heavily class structured, and most people end up in jobs in which they have little opportunity to actualize their human potential. Daily frustration, stress, and alienation are internalized in the form of self-blame, which is then brought home, where it explodes in ways that weaken families and make friendships and relationships much less stable. These dynamics are discussed more thoroughly in my book, *Surplus Powerlessness: The Psychodynamics of Daily Life and the Psychology of Individual and Social Transformation* (Humanities Press, 1991), and in the pages of *Tikkun* magazine.

Many Americans are in a great deal of pain in their daily lives, but what they hear from the Left often seems to imply that their pain is irrelevant, that the only *real* pain is the pain of the *most oppressed* (Blacks, women, gays, the handicapped, people with AIDS, etc.). Many of these people turn to the Right because the Right seems to acknowledge that there is something wrong in people's lives (even if it then goes on unfairly to blame gays, the women's movement, liberals, or some other scapegoat, instead of looking at the way the competitive society that the Right supports has played a major role in generating the problems).

This is a perfect opportunity for leftists to enter the arena and explain why much of the pain people are feeling has to do not with their own personal failures but with the consequences of a certain kind of social organization and the values it generates. But to unpack these self-blaming dynamics in the rest of the society, to generate a mass psychology of compassion, the leftists would first have to let go of self-blaming in their own lives. And they find this very difficult to do.

Jews on the Left are one segment of the problem, and they would be making an important contribution to the whole process if they could let go of their self-blaming, accept themselves as Jews, and accept the weaknesses and distortions in Jewish life with an appropriate level of compassion. Not that Jews should not still struggle against the misguided policies of the State of Israel; on the contrary, that struggle would be stronger and more effective if it came out of love and not self-hatred and self-denigration. One place to start in this whole process would be for Jews on the Left to take an aggressive role in confronting anti-Semitism, and also to confront the self-hating Jews on the Left in a loving way .

Unfortunately, in order to start even the most loving and compassionate process one must sometimes be confrontational. Nothing was better for the Left, for example, than for women to insist that sexism on the Left had to stop, and for them to make this demand in ways that confronted sexist practices, sexist men, and sexist women. The hardest part for feminist women, of course, was having to deal with other women who denied that there was any real problem of sexism within the Left. We need an analogous process in combating anti-Semitism in the Left.

There are three parts of the process that need to go on simultaneously:

1. **Education Within the Left about Anti-Semitism.** Jewish activists should urge every liberal or progressive social change organization they are part of or are sympathetic with to institute an internal education program. This book was written in part to be used as a component of such an internal self-education. No group in the liberal and progressive camps—local chapters of the Democratic party, organizations concerned with the environment, health care, women's issues, gay issues, homelessness, peace, social justice, human rights, unions, liberal think-tanks, alternative press, radio, television, liberal associations of doctors, lawyers, social workers, teachers, therapists—should be exempt from this kind of self-reflection and self-education. Jews on the Left should be raising this demand to all of the relevant institutions, no matter how clogged their schedules, no matter how preoccupied their activists.

2. **Consciousness-Raising Groups for Jews Who Are Part of the Social-Change Movements.** Jews on the Left can form support groups that explicitly consider questions of Jewishness and anti-Semitism, and the way these issues arise within the movements for social change, within the larger society, and within ourselves. Like the small consciousness-raising groups of the women's movement, these groups should deal with both with internal and personal issues, and with helping individuals to be more effective agents of social change. Some of these groups have already begun to use articles from *Tikkun* and the *Tikkun Anthology,* and others might use this book as a basis for some initial discussion.

Part of the consciousness-raising process requires a rethinking of your own life, your family and how its seemingly idiosyncratic dynamics were partially shaped by centuries of Jewish oppression and by centuries of Jewish strengths. We at *Tikkun* are trying to train some psychotherapists with the relevant skills and knowledge to be

An activist demonstrates against Israel at an antiwar rally protesting U.S. intervention in the Gulf.

ble to assist in this work. Despite the fact that psychoanalytic tradiions emphasize reclaiming the repressed memories of the past, a disproportionate number of Jewish therapists have managed to avoid dealing with their own Jewishness, have little understanding of how their families absorbed Jewish self-hatred, and hence are often ill-equipped to help others think these issues through.

3. **Disruption of Anti-Semitic Activity and Talk on the Left.** While I've been writing this book, by chance three different people have told me of incidents in which someone they were out with on a date made some anti-Semitic comment, not knowing that they were Jewish. In all three cases, the Jewish person simply said nothing, each assuring me that they would never see the other person again but that they did not want to cause a scene by confronting them right on the spot. Imagine how much harder it will be when the issue isn't some typically anti-Semitic remark, but behavior that involves anti-Semitic Israel-bashing or other instances of anti-Semitism that I've described here. And yet, in this case, we want to prevent people from never having another "date" with the Left. Publicly confronting anti-Semitism on the Left may be the only thing that will force a change.

For example, imagine yourself at a teach-in or public meeting critiquing some aspect of American foreign policy. Many people participated in something like this during the Gulf War. Suddenly, in the midst of a talk about what's wrong with Bush and his policies, a speaker makes a comment about how Bush's policies serve the Zionist plan, or how "the Jewish lobby" has maneuvered us into the war, or the speaker suddenly focuses on what's wrong with Israel. Your task is to get up in the middle of that talk and say clearly and calmly, "I didn't come here to hear anti-Jewish racism parading as progressive politics. Stop that garbage and deal with the issue." If someone else has already done that, your task is to get up and support them. It is not sufficient if *after* the meeting you go over to someone who complained about anti-Semitism and say, "I'm glad you said that." Rather, get up on the spot and say what you have to say publicly. Ideally, you will know other Jews or non-Jews who recognize the need to fight anti-Semitism and who may be going to the same event. Call them on the phone beforehand and tell them that you want their public support should you face anti-Semitic remarks or inferences at the public gathering.

Eventually, you need to develop a support group of others who will plan to take action together. Rather than simply making a short and dismissable statement, the group should agree to go to the platform, perhaps carrying placards saying "No to anti-Semitism,"

"There's no room for Jew-hating in a liberal or progressive movement," or something of the sort.

The goal is not to disrupt the speakers. On the contrary, our commitment to free speech means that the only kind of anti-Semitism that should be completely disrupted is that kind in which the speaker is urging acts of violence against Jews. We are far from that at the moment, though the recent electoral strength of ex-Nazi David Duke suggests that by the end of the twentieth century we might well see overt anti-Semitic movements on the Right that will be even more serious than the relatively contained variety on the Left. While we ought not prevent a speaker from finishing, we ought to be able to express collective disapproval during a speech (boos, shouting negative remarks) just as people show collective approval with cheers or clapping.

When a speaker is engaging in anti-Semitism, you and your friends should go to the platform, stage, or podium and demand time to present an on-the-spot analysis of the speaker's anti-Semitism.

This is the hardest part and requires the greatest breakthrough in our internalized oppression as Jews. Jews are used to being targets, and one of the ways we've learned to protect ourselves is to make ourselves inconspicuous *as Jews* (at least in our own self-conception, although others still think of us as conspicuously Jewish). So it will be hard for Jews to stand up as Jews and say, "We are tired of both covert and overt anti-Semitism on the Left and we won't let it continue unchallenged."

Of course, the first group that will oppose those Jews who do stand up and attack anti-Semitism will be the Jewish self-haters on the Left. One way that they can be dealt with is to be as obnoxious toward them as they are toward you—calling them Uncle Toms or Uncle Maxes or whatever, confronting their self-hating attitudes, or drawing analogies to those who took a similar attitude when feminism or black consciousness appeared in the movement. Another method is to invite them to a Jewish consciousness-raising group in which they get a chance to talk out some of the issues with you.

Creating a Jewish Left Organization

Just as women and Blacks felt it necessary to have specifically feminist and Black liberation–oriented organizations, so it may be necessary at some moments for Jews to form a Jewish Left organization. Yet separating Jews from the mainstream of liberal and progressive organizations, while it may at times be necessary in order to provide a climate of safety in which Jews can explore how to be both Jewish and progressive, could have the consequence of further accelerating the centrifugal tendencies on the Left, and further complicate efforts to build a renewed universalism that can overcome all the various particularisms that currently flourish.

Our solution was to create the Committee for Judaism and Social Justice as a kind of cadre organization—a small group of people who share a common perspective who will both meet and support one another as Jews, but also coordinate and mutually support one another when we work in larger mass organizations of the progressive world. Rather than attempting to create a *mass* organization that is an alternative locus for political activity, CJSJ works within the liberal and progressive movements, but does so as a group of self-affirming Jews. CJSJ's primary goals—to change the Jewish world to make it more focused on the struggle for social justice (both in the U.S. and Israel) and also to change the progressive movements to make them more sensitive to Jewish issues and to move them from a focus on the politics of entitlements and rights to the politics of meaning—allow us to function as a coherent group with a shared worldview, and yet to participate in the larger frameworks of social-change organizations.

Inevitably, there will be those who reject the notion of a Jewish cadre working together to advance our goals, and who will say that this is unnecessary or sectarian or "splitting the Left." These objections are reasonable only if the very people who raise them raise similar objections to African Americans, women, gays and lesbians, and any other group that has formed separate caucuses or organizations to meet their needs.

What Should Non-Jews Do to Fight Anti-Semitism on the Left?

Confronting anti-Semitism and marginalizing the self-hating Jews in the movement in order to make it possible for self-affirming Jews to feel welcome should not be a task only for Jews. Non-Jews have as much responsibility to deal with this issue as men have to deal with the issue of sexism.

Here are some guidelines:

- Don't wait for Jews to raise the issue. Raise it yourself. From the reactions you get from Jews you'll immediately know who is a self-affirmer and who is a self-denier.

- Create an internal education program for these issues. Encourage friends, co-workers, members of your church or community center, and people with whom you do political work to read and discuss this book.

- Disrupt anti-Semitic comments or speakers, and support Jews when they do so. Interfere with attempts to include Jews in the category "white," with the implicit assumption that Jews are *not* oppressed.

- Put self-affirming Jews in positions of leadership in your organizations. When seeking ethnic diversity and balance, explicitly include Jews as one of the categories to be recognized. Of course, Jews already play a role in some liberal and progressive social-change movements that is disproportionate to their numbers in the population. These Jews get into positions of leadership not because they are Jews, but despite that fact. As a result, those who advance are often those who are most able to play down their Jewishness, and these tend to be the self-deniers rather than the self-affirmers. These are precisely the people who are likely to dismiss the notion that Jews are oppressed or that the history or current reality of Jew-hating deserves consideration.

Liberal and progressive social-change movements need to have self-affirming Jews in positions of leadership. Just as the Left would be reluctant to have as spokespeople a group of women who were antifeminist, or African Americans who thought that attention to oppression of Blacks was being "exaggerated" in America, so also the Left must avoid Jewish leaders who do not understand the history and current reality of anti-Semitism or who do not understand why many Jews have felt pushed away by the Left.

Do not ignore the problem or think it will go away. It won't—it will reassert itself in more vicious forms. After decades of squandering money on the military, the U.S. economy is significantly weakened, and its ability to compete in the world economic market has been severely shaken. The ecological crisis will further limit the ways American corporations can make profits. In a world that will have to be tightening its belt, there will be a renewed sympathy for those who find scapegoats. The remarkable phenomenon of anti-Semitism in Japan—a society where there are almost no Jews—testifies to the ability of one society to adopt another's scapegoats. Jews are likely once again to be scapegoats in various places around the world.

Moreover, this irrational hatred of Jews will be fueled by the degree to which people around the world unfairly blame the entire Jewish people for the Israeli government's antidemocratic and repressive actions against Palestinians. While racism and Jew-hating are never justified, the justifiable anger that people feel at Israeli policy will tend to give anti-Semites a "rational cover" for their hateful attitudes.

All the more reason that liberal and progressive social-change movements need to be intellectually armed and prepared to counter anti-Semitism. But this cannot happen unless they have *already* dealt with their own anti-Semitism. That's why it's so important to confront anti-Semitism in the liberal and progressive movements *now*.

There is another reason. Anti-Semitism weakens the Left and turns away many potential allies.

Most polls indicate that Jews share liberal and progressive ideas to a higher extent than virtually any other ethnic group. Yet Jews often feel alienated and pushed away by the Left. Those who care about building progressive social-change movements have to care about fighting anti-Semitism, not only because it's morally right, but also because in order to win the struggles for peace, social justice, environmental sanity, equality, and human dignity, liberal and progressive Jews need to be part of the relevant movements. To the extent that you push Jews away, or make it harder for self-affirming Jews to take positions of leadership in your organizations, you undermine your own cause. Avoiding the issue of anti-Semitism, or allowing self-denying or self-hating Jews to set the tone for how Jews are going to be dealt with in liberal and progressive social-change movements, is not only immoral, it is also self-destructive.

9
Anti-Semitism in the African-American Community

One of the saddest developments in American progressive politics in the past few decades has been the growing estrangement between the African American and Jewish communities. The powerful assault on random Jews in Crown Heights—including the murder of one Jew as an act of "retaliation" against the accidental slaying of two children by a Chasidic driver who lost control of his car—was only the visible expression of a deep and abiding antagonism that can no longer be ignored. Jews on campuses of many universities report that they sometimes hear African-American visiting lecturers using code words about Jews that have a long history associated with Jew-hating. And when these Jewish students complain, they are too often faced with silence or complicity by responsible African-American leaders. In truth, the number of incidents is relatively small, but, given the history of Jewish oppression, they are taken very seriously by many Jews and contribute to a deepening alienation between Blacks and Jews.

True, tensions also exist between Blacks and a variety of other communities, particularly Asians, who have increasingly replaced Jews in their role as shopkeepers and landlords. Yet there is a special poignancy to the Black-Jewish antagonism, in part because so many liberal Jews have been involved in activism or in providing political and financial help to the civil-rights movement. When many Jews think about liberal or progressive politics, their first association is the struggle for civil rights, and their second is the struggle for economic justice (which *also* tends to involve the interests of Blacks and other Third World communities). For many Jews, then, the discovery of anti-Semitism in these communities *is* functionally identical to discovering anti-Semitism on the Left.

117

Sources of Tension

Jews lived in the ghettos and slums of the central cities when they first came to the U.S., and in the process of moving up the economic ladder many of them became small shopkeepers and landlords. As Jews eventually made enough money, they were able to move out of the central city, first to more desirable locations in the city itself, then to the suburbs. It was often Blacks, as well as Puerto Ricans, Cubans, and Dominicans on the East Coast, and Chicanos on the West Coast, who moved into these same areas as Jews moved out. For these minorities, daily life experience often involved dealing with the Jewish grocer, the Jewish clothing store or department store owner, or the Jewish landlord. For Jews, the experience of Eastern Europe was being repeated—Jews as "the public face" of capitalism for another group of oppressed people.

The children of the shopkeepers and landlords often sought entry into American society in a different way—by becoming the most respected members of "the helping professions." As teachers, social workers, doctors, lawyers, psychologists, and government bureaucrats, a large number of Jews found a way to combine their own desire to "make the world a better place" with a desire to achieve status and economic security (or in some cases prosperity). Many of these Jewish professionals were self-consciously committed to progressive ideals and social change. Rather than leave their ideals to their personal lives, they sought ways to embody in their daily lives their commitment to justice and equality.

Unfortunately, the actual operations of the legal, educational, governmental, and health bureaucracies often work in ways that are not perceived by the poorest and most oppressed sections of the society as "real service." On the contrary, many often feel that these social services are instruments of oppression, ways in which the dominant society distributes the minimum amount of services necessary to prevent outright revolt, and are inadequate to allow the recipients either human dignity or a real opportunity to change their circumstances. Many of the institutions that provide services to the most oppressed do have a mixed impact.

On the one hand, no one can deny that these institutions do deliver necessary services, and that, in fact, the lives of many African Americans, Puerto Ricans, Chicanos, and others would be considerably worse if these services were not available. On the other hand,

Confrontations in the Crown Heights section of Brooklyn highlighted the current tension between the Jewish and African-American communities.

and often despite the best intentions of the service deliverers, the way these bureaucracies work in practice often reconfirms and intensifies the powerlessness of many of their clients and beneficiaries. All too often, particularly in the areas that are home to Third World groups, Jews have had a disproportionate role in these institutions. Many Third World people have concluded that Jews are the responsible party, not the larger wealthy and powerful elites who actually control these institutions and determine what resources to make available.

Grievances: Legitimate and Illegitimate

Jews in the helping professions or in social service contexts in which they are delivering badly needed social supports, services, or education to African-American communities sometimes feel that they are the butt of an inexplicable and irrational anti-Semitism. Rarely understanding the social context that generates the anger among those who are receiving the social services, Jews feel that they are facing hostility that confirms their worst fears—that anti-Semitism will always be there, regardless of what they do and no matter how hard they try. Coupled with the political disillusionment that developed after the civil-rights movement, many Jews now feel skeptical about the struggle for Black rights and entitlements and feel that all they've offered is unappreciated and scorned; Jews too feel angry, but it's a response to the rejection.

There is no doubt that some interactions between Jews and Blacks follow a classic racist pattern. Some Jews, serving in positions of authority over Blacks, have acted in authoritarian, exploitative or oppressive manners. Yet their Jewishness has nothing to do with this behavior. The previous history of Jewish oppression helped determine that Jews would fill some of the social roles as minor-league oppressors; but for Blacks to focus on the *Jewishness* of the people in these roles is as racist as for whites to focus on the *Blackness* of poor people who in the desperation of poverty have been driven to engage in criminal behavior. The willingness to generalize from the behavior of some to the larger group to which they belong is illegitimate and a classic characteristic of racism.

The shock that many Jews feel in facing Black anti-Semitism is sometimes disingenuous to the extent that it represents a refusal to acknowledge legitimate grievances some Blacks have against some Jews who are acting *as Jews*. The role of the American Jewish Committee and other Jewish establishment organizations in opposing racial quotas designed to achieve equality for Blacks in employment was taken by many Blacks as symbolic of the insensitivity of the Jewish community toward Black aspirations. But for Jews, the very notion of "quota" brought back the experience, not so far in the historical past, in which Jews had been kept out of jobs and educational opportunities because of anti-Jewish quotas. Yet Blacks quite persuasively argued that in the last decades of the twentieth century in America Jews were so vastly overrepresented in educational and professional institutions that they should not worry about some measures aimed at rectifying past discrimination against Blacks. I support their argument here, just as I support the position of Zionists who argue for the continuation of the Law of Return in Israel that allows Jews an automatic right to citizenship that is not granted to others.

It is easy to understand why educated Blacks—those who were seeking entry into educational and professional institutions—felt most offended by what was perceived as *official Jewish opposition* to affirmative action. On the other hand, to generalize to *all Jews* again misses the nuances in the Jewish world. After all, there were many

Jews who not only supported affirmative action but who were actually in the vanguard of the struggle for Third World studies programs and for the acceptance of the principle of affirmative action. It seemed insensitive at best for some Black intellectuals to ignore the role of the Jewish Left, and to pay attention only to those on the Jewish Right.

Insensitivity, however, is *not* the same as anti-Semitism. And in this instance, African-American intellectuals are responding to official Jewish institutions claiming to be speaking for the entire Jewish people that are acting in ways that are offensive to Blacks. To be angry at Jews for the behavior of their official institutions is legitimate, even if misguided.

Jewish Racism Toward Blacks

Jews are often unwilling to acknowledge the extent to which racist attitudes toward Blacks have become a part of American Jewish life. Like virtually every other group in America, Jews accepted racist stereotypes about Blacks, and crude humor about "shvartzes" attests to this attitude. Blacks who served as housekeepers or employees of Jews were sometimes invisible to these Jews; racist attitudes that existed in some sectors of the Jewish world were expressed freely, and the reports of these attitudes certainly impressed many Blacks, intensifying an already existing anger toward Jews.

In short, Jews were not innocent bystanders. Then again, no one implicated in a world of oppression is totally innocent. That some Africans engaged in the slave trade and were involved in selling their fellow Blacks to slave-traders does nothing to mitigate white racism. There have been some Jewish racists, but this fact can never justify generalized antagonism toward all members of the Jewish people by some Blacks.

Nevertheless, Jews have become accepted members of the larger white society and therefore have, by and large, participated in and benefited from economic arrangements that exploit Blacks and place Jews in a position of moral vulnerability. There is a fundamental asymmetry in the relationship of Blacks to Jews because Blacks have been systematically excluded from the privileges of American society, while Jews have had the same opportunities as most other non-ruling-class Americans. Just as I argued that Palestinians, by virtue of participating in the larger Islamic culture and proudly claiming their role in the Arab nation, have some real responsibility for the long history of oppression of Jews in Arab lands, so too Jews who have been able to prosper in a racist society have some responsibility for the oppression of Blacks. A Jewish commitment to end racism toward Blacks should not be conceived as an act of largess by a group that was not implicated in the oppression, but rather as a moral necessity on the part of a group that has been spared the worst impact of the fluctuations of the capitalist market, precisely because in America the worst impact is distributed disproportionately to Blacks.

This fundamental asymmetry is *not,* however, a warrant for anti-Semitism. The "socialism of fools" that leads many Blacks to believe that their real enemy is the Jew and to misunderstand the real nature of their oppression is *not* an excusable mistake. For Jews who watched demagogues in Europe turn prejudice among the uneducated peasantry and working classes into a deadly campaign of extermination, the prospect of a growing Black anti-Semitism generates legitimate concern and anger.

Multiculturalism

In the late 1960s and 1970s, many Jews on the Left played an important role in demanding that universities, publishing houses, the media, and other cultural and intellectual institutions open their doors to reflect a diversity of intellectual and cultural traditions that had been previously ignored. Jews on the Left played a leadership role in these struggles, but rarely demanded that Jewish culture and Jewish history be included in the newly emerging diversity.

Jews can be proud of having been supporters of this struggle. Yet some of the results have been hurtful to Jewish interests and concerns. In some of the contexts in which multiculturalism has been espoused and taken seriously, there has simultaneously developed a climate of antagonism toward Jews and Israel.

Jews complain that multiculturalism has sometimes gone hand in hand with the following developments:

• A facile identification of Jews with Zionism, and Zionism with the oppressive policies of the current government of Israel.

•A double standard in judging Israel. Legitimate criticisms of Israel's providing arms to various oppressive regimes are made without a similar focus on countries like China, Russia, France, or Germany that have sold arms and equipment to help bolster repressive regimes. Similarly, correct criticisms of human-rights abuses in Israel are matched by an inexcusable silence about human-rights abuses that take place in many African and Third World countries, unless the abuses can be blamed on some association with Israel or Western powers.

•The tendency to view Jews as "white" and as part of the colonial or imperialist elite oppressing Third World nations. The long history of Jewish oppression, and the callous disregard for Jewish fate by Third World countries and movements during the Holocaust, is ignored and largely unknown. The linguistic move of substituting "people of color" for "oppressed minorities," coupled with the decision to refer to Jews as "whites," becomes an anti-Semitic denial of Jewish history.

•Jewish literature, long ignored in the universities, is now excluded from the new agenda of multiculturalism, and Jewish history, totally denied or obscured by whites, is now itself excluded as white.

Remedies

As Third World people become a major part of the population of America's most populous states, the antagonism toward Jews in some Third World communities may become even more important and potentially dangerous. And the long-predicted economic decline of the U.S. (based in part on the stupidity of right-wing policies that sunk trillions of dollars into war-related production instead of into the economic infrastructure necessary to make America competitive in the marketplaces of the twenty-first century) may generate new pressures for a scapegoat. It is not inconceivable that African Americans in alliance with other Third World groups will be too numerous and too powerful to serve safely as scapegoats for the declining ruling elite. Instead, some sectors of the ruling elite will once again turn to focus on the Jews, this time with the active support of some sectors of the Third World population.

There is nothing inevitable about this scenario, but we cannot disregard it. Rather, it is imperative for progressive movements to address and combat the issue of anti-Semitism in Third World communities, making it a high priority in the future.

I asked Jesse Jackson to join *Tikkun* in projecting a joint campaign against racism in both our communities. Though Mr. Jackson did not accept the offer, I believe this idea can point us in the most plausible direction: one that acknowledges the problems in *both* communities, avoids placing blame on one or the other group, and mobilizes people in both communities to address the joint danger.

Education to combat racism must avoid the pitfalls of the "interfaith dialogue" that was developed in the U.S. to smooth relations between Christians and Jews. All too often, these dialogues become little more than encounters between professional "make-nice" people (community relations officials) whose job is to accentuate the positive rather than seriously explore the points of tension. A real dialogue between these communities must seek to bring churches and synagogues together, to bring poor Blacks into contact with Jewish groups (including groups of Jews who identify with liberal and progressive causes), and to share, in an honest way, positive feelings, angers, and misunderstandings. Only in safe environments can people feel free to speak about their anger and hope that they can achieve some kind of real understanding that allows them to move beyond that anger.

Important work in building alliances is being done by the National Coalition-Building Institute in Washington, D.C., under the leadership of Cherie Brown. Her work brings Blacks and Jews together to explore how racist and anti-Semitic attitudes have been deeply internalized, and how to uncover these attitudes and struggle against them.

The Committee for Judaism and Social Justice is also involved in various educational projects aimed at "unlearning racism," in the words of the late Ricky Marcuse-Sherover. CJSJ chapters approach Third World studies programs, Black and Chicano churches, Asian community centers, and a variety of community organizations that speak to, and for, Third World communities, and ask them to set up opportunities for CJSJ members to make presentations about anti-Semitism. CJSJ chapters spark heated and often transformative dialogues with Third World people who have been sitting on a mass of unspoken feelings about Jews, some of them based on double standards or simple misconceptions. At the same time, these dialogues have been useful in that they allow us and members of the Jewish community to learn more about the feelings and perspectives of many Third World people. Criticisms that may have seemed anti-Semitic when learned about only through the media sometimes turn out to be quite legitimate when Jews hear them articulated in person.

Confronting Black Anti-Semitism

Jews have much to learn by listening to African Americans and other Third World communities; we also have much to do to clean up our own act and fight our own racism toward Blacks and others. The unfortunate truth, however, is that other victims of racism sometimes have racist attitudes toward Jews. Black anti-Semitism cannot be completely reduced to justified anger at Jews. The climate of anti-Semitic attitudes and ideas that has reasserted itself in recent years requires that Jews confront and struggle against these manifestations of Jew-hating.

But confronting Black anti-Semitism is particularly difficult for liberal and progressive Jews. One major reason is the overwhelming guilt Jews feel about the oppression Third World people have experienced. As I said above, that guilt is not wholly inappropriate in that Jews have participated in the benefits of the larger society and therefore share some of the responsibility for the oppression that is built into its normal workings. Jews have benefited from racism; many Jews have made racist statements, told racist jokes, and shared racist attitudes.

Nevertheless, Jews are neither the creators nor the major beneficiaries of racism toward Blacks, and Jews have played a major role in trying to alleviate some of the worst effects of racism. Blacks have a right to live in a world without racism, and so, too, do Jews. So when Jews experience anti-Semitism in Third World communities or among Third World intellectuals, they have a right and duty to confront it, even though it stems from those who also are oppressed.

Why a duty? Because we have the duty to help end the oppression of African Americans, a duty that is necessarily impeded by Black anti-Semitism.

This last point deserves elaboration. One of the destructive elements of "liberal guilt" is that it disempowers liberals to act as *real* allies to the people whom they ought to be supporting. I experienced this first-hand as an activist in the New Left in the 1960s: White radicals often refused to confront their Black allies or attempt to dissuade them from self-destructive activity, because, they reasoned, "Who are we to tell these people who have suffered so much what's in their best interest?" Let me recount one dramatic incident. A group of activists in the Students for a Democratic Society (SDS) attended a meeting of the leadership of the Black Panthers. The Panthers were planning a "United Front Against Fascism," and the question arose of what would happen if a group of people from the Trotskyite Socialist Workers Party attempted to use the occasion to advance their own line at this event. "We'll 'off' them," said Panther leader Bobby Seale (as in the Panther phrase "off the Pigs," which was generally understood to mean kill them). I objected and told Seale that I thought he shouldn't be saying that kind of thing, even as a joke. After all, I argued, these people may be misguided, but they don't deserve to die, and we have no right to use violence against them. Afterward, a movement leader was furious at me for having dared to confront the esteemed leader of the Black Panthers. He warned me that I was endangering the whole relationship between Blacks and whites, and excluded me from future meetings. Seale was no murderer; I knew he didn't mean what he was saying. But I wasn't sure that others around him understood that he was merely posturing. Later, Seale was arrested for murder in New Haven, allegedly for ordering the deaths of certain enemies of the Panthers. I could easily imagine that his words had been misunderstood—and I felt angry at other activists who had not stood with me in urging Seale to change the way he talked. In fact, it was precisely this use of violent language that enabled the police to use violence against the Panthers and get away with it. White liberal supporters felt that they didn't have the right to challenge the Panthers when they were doing something destructive, and our failure to be real comrades hurt the Panthers.

Similarly, Jews and non-Jews who do not actively confront Black anti-Semitism are actually doing a disservice to Third World communities. In this case, confronting anti-Semitism is not just self-serving. It is also serving the interests of human liberation.

But there is a second reason many Jews are reluctant to confront anti-Semitism in Third World communities. On many college campuses, where the conflicts between Jews and Blacks have at times been particularly intense, Jews have reported that when they *have* challenged anti-Semitic remarks from Blacks, they have encountered an anger that borders on violence, or suggests that violence might follow soon. I have questioned Jews who make these reports to determine whether their perceptions may have been based more on racist stereotypes about Blacks than on real experience. However, after listening to many stories and asking critical and skeptical questions, I am convinced that some of these perceptions may be legitimate. As in any political struggle where emotions run high, there is sometimes the threat of a violent eruption.

For most intellectuals, it might seem easier to avoid the situation entirely. For many Jews, it is easier to identify with these expressions of anger, to find political legitimation for what is sometimes a clearly anti-Semitic eruption, and therefore to free oneself from the necessity of confronting it.

But allowing our behavior to be influenced by the perceived threat of violence could be a major mistake for Jews. In his book *People in Trouble,* Wilhelm Reich tells a frightening story of the rise of fascism in Germany in the 1920s. According to Reich, one of the ways the fascist movement managed to win power was by physically intimidating other political parties that were much larger than the Fascist party. A central part of their fascist strategy was to use violence in demonstrations on the streets and to confront peaceful demonstrators with the choice of engaging in violence or ceding the streets to them. Overwhelmingly, the leftists chose to cede the streets rather than fight. This provided a major psychological victory for the fascists, who then were able to inspire in people a growing fear of participating in the Left. The lesson here is that Jews specifically, and leftists in general, may have to band together in ways that provide one another with the physical safety to confront anti-Semitism publicly.

The notion of Jewish self-defense has taken only two forms in the past decades: either aliya to Israel, where people could feel physically secure behind Israeli military power, or joining various right-wing militant groups like the late Rabbi Kahane's Jewish Defense League. But we are entering a period in which we need left-wing organizations for Jewish defense—so that individual Jews who face the choice of whether to confront anti-Semitism will feel that they have the necessary support to do so.

Unlike right-wing defense organizations, a left-wing defense organization would not seek to exacerbate differences between Jews and other ethnic communities but would rather be committed to providing mutual support. For example, during the recent surge of anti-Arab violence, people at the Committee for Judaism and Social Justice proposed that we provide protection for Arab stores and get Arab organizations to provide security at vulnerable Jewish sites. Jewish defense work can build bridges to other communities— even if its bottom line is protection of Jews as they confront anti-Semitism in the U.S.

The greatest danger to Jews lies not in the anger of Third World communities, but in the racism that is a traditional part of right-wing movements. David Duke's success in winning 55 percent of the white votes in Louisiana in a 1991 election shows how real this danger might be. Jews may well need a militant self-defense organization that can address this danger on the Right. All the more reason for Jews to confront the problems on the Left, so that these problems can be addressed and Jews can more firmly establish their ties to liberal and progressive social-change movements.

I believe that the failure to confront Black and other Third World progressive leaders about the growing anti-Semitism within their movements is a dangerous mistake that can only lead to greater pain in those communities. Jews do not have the great power that some conspiracy theorists claim. But they do have some positions of influence, and should use those positions to advance the needs of the poor and oppressed. As such, liberal Jews can counterbalance the growing willingness of many other sectors of society, including some sectors of the Black community, to throw up their hands and relinquish all efforts to deal with the problems of the most heavily oppressed sectors of the Black community. With phrases such as "the culture of the underclass," dominant white elites tend to blame the oppressed for the poverty, homelessness, and hunger that disproportionately fall on Third World communities in the U.S. While a sensitive ally must validate the need of Blacks to focus more attention on creating cultural alternatives and models for a different lifestyle than the macho and sexist vision sometimes validated in rap music, it must also be in a position to counter the blame-the-victim mentality that is fostered by contemporary apologia for capitalism's worst excesses. The Jews are well-positioned to be that ally. But they can't serve as an ally if they feel so threatened by anti-Semitic overtones in the Black community that they feel safer staying away from Blacks altogether. People who care about the future welfare of the Black community must urge it to do all it can to oppose anti-Semitism publicly, and begin to work as allies for Jews in liberal and progressive social-change movements.

Jews, on the other hand, must do all they can to avoid the trap of waiting for Blacks to prove themselves free of all vestiges of anti-Semitism before they are willing to support African-American struggles. The oppression that Blacks continue to experience in a racist society is outrageous. Black outrage and rioting in the Spring of 1992 after the acquittal of four policemen in Los Angeles who had been videotaped as they viciously beat a Black man briefly reminded the nation that the long legacy of racism remains a daily reality for many African Americans. It would be foolish indeed if Jews were to focus exclusively on the pathology of anti-Semitism in the Black community without understanding that these kinds of pathology are an inevitable outgrowth of oppression. And when people are in pain, it is often those who are closest to them, not those who are their real enemies, who get subjected to their anger and abuse. The best way to stop the anger and abuse is to change the social system that has allowed America's cities to decay, allowed Blacks to be last hired and first fired, allowed people to go without adequate health care or housing or food, and has generated a societal-wide sense of isolation and loneliness so deep that people are ready to grab on to simplistic and racist explanations of their pain.

To recognize the legitimacy of Black anger, to refuse those moves which try to blame the victim and pretend that the only problem is the "culture of poverty," should be a central part of a Jewish response. But Jews should insist that they will not accept inappropriate anger and abuse, even as they work for changing social conditions. I've encountered some Jews on the Left who are so full of righteous indignation at the oppression faced by Blacks that they are incapable of recognizing the Jew-hating that sometimes goes on in Black communities and even among progressive Blacks. In the long run, their uncritical stance does not really serve the interests of African Americans. I imagine that some of these people will be attacking this book, insisting that there really is no problem of Jew-hating worth considering. All the more reason why those Jews who can think more complexly and recognize that raising these issues is not a sign of disloyalty or lack of caring need to stick together. Using this book as one vehicle for focusing discussion, they need to create small consciousness-raising groups in which the issue of anti-Semitism on the Left can be more fully explored, and in which they can plan how to support each other in raising these questions publicly in the liberal and progressive world. Doing so will take a great deal of courage—and a willingness to risk being labeled and discounted by some on the Left.

Conclusion

Ultimately, progressive Jews have no choice but to confront these issues head-on. Those who fail to do so will guarantee their political irrelevance. Fewer and fewer Jews will feel safe in a political context that pretends to overlook anti-Semitism. If the Left does not free its ranks of anti-Semitism, more and more Jews will embrace the Right and its analysis of anti-Semitism as a kind of ontological fact of Jewish existence that makes it impossible to trust non-Jews.

Anti-Semitism is a misguided and defeatable position. We reject the notion that the goyim* are so gullible and evil that they will always be manipulable into anti-Semitic ideas. On the contrary, in our view non-Jews who have adopted racist ideas can be won to a non-racist view of the world.

The socialism of fools can be defeated—though it will take a sustained campaign of education, confrontation, and self-examination. Central to this campaign are the following:

1. **Understanding the particular nature of Jewish oppression**—the way that Jews are set up in positions in which they appear to have power and can thus become targets when the oppression built into the social system generates anger that can no longer be controlled by the elites of wealth and power. Implicit in this recognition is the central truth of Jewish existence: Jewish survival requires the elimination of systems of oppression. There can be no solution to our problems without a larger tikkun, a larger healing, repair, and transformation of the world. Jewish destiny requires that Jews be engaged in changing the world. Yet the larger healing and transformation cannot be accomplished until, and unless, all forms and vestiges of anti-

---

*Though in Yiddish this term sometimes acquired negative connotations, in the traditional liturgy the word 'goy' continues to be used in reference to the people of Israel, a holy people, *goy kadosh.*

Semitism are understood and explicitly fought against by those seeking to repair the world.

2. **Providing support and encouragement to Jews to learn their own history and culture, to reclaim what is liberatory and healing within it, and to positively affirm their Jewishness.** Such affirmation does not require uncritical acceptance of all aspects of Judaism or Jewish culture. It does require a compassionate attitude toward the Jewish people, an understanding of *how* the distortions in our consciousness and in our culture may have been engendered, and a willingness to accept lovingly the limitations of our own people, our own families, and ourselves, and then to extend that same loving and compassionate attitude to non-Jews. Such a process requires a serious commitment to learning about Jewish history, literature, philosophy, religion, and culture—and also a deep psychological process of re-understanding oneself, one's relationship to fellow Jews and non-Jews, one's family and its relationship to the history of Jewish oppression, and Israel and its relationship to the history of Jewish pain. This kind of work can best be done in Jewish consciousness-raising groups.

3. **Allowing ourselves to overcome the tendency toward "goyim-bashing" and pessimism about the possibility of ever being able to fully trust non-Jews.** The knee-jerk distrust of the non-Jew, built on a solid basis of historical evidence, much like the chauvinist interpretations of Jewish chosenness, is an understandable reaction to a long history of oppression. It is my belief that we live in a very different historical period, one in which it is truly possible to build trusting and safe relationships with the non-Jewish world. A paranoid attitude toward others, a sense that non-Jews will always act in selfish or destructive ways, is too often a self-fulfilling prophecy. Our strategy for breaking this cycle must include the following caveats:

a. Trust does not require pretending that the past didn't happen. On the contrary, it is precisely because we trust that non-Jews *can* be allies for the Jews that we are willing to take the risk of insisting that they consciously and publicly deal with the long history of anti-Semitism, and that they *act as allies* by confronting anti-Semitism wherever they find it, including in self-hating Jews. Pushing non-Jews on these issues is a sign of caring and openness, just as confronting a life-partner or child about something that is making you distant is a sign of affirming your desire for the relationship.

b. Trusting the possibility that non-Jews can be our allies is not naive, nor is it a guarantee that all non-Jews will be allies. Nor can we rule out the resurgence of irrational anti-Semitism such as we now see in Eastern Europe and Japan. For that reason, fighting goyim-bashing in the Jewish world does *not* require that we give up our vigilance on the issue of anti-Semitism. Israel should be strong and capable of defending itself. For the foreseeable future, the Jewish people are going to need an army—at least until thirty or forty other countries take the lead and disarm *first*. But Israel should not be so paranoid about the inevitability of the world being against it that it does not take advantage of the actual openings for peace that exist. It would be self-destructive for Israel to act in cynical and manipulative ways that generate the very antagonism that the pessimists predict.

Unlike previous generations of leftists and liberals who thought the best solution to racism would be to eliminate all forms of particularity, we believe that particular ethnic traditions can make important contributions. The best kind of world is not one in which there is a homogenized, universal culture, but rather a community of dialogue between many different cultures. We are all too aware that preserving ethnicity may also mean preserving a history of racism or vicious nationalism toward others. Hence we need to qualify our support for "difference" and for the plethora of cultural traditions by saying that we support those traditions to the extent that they are themselves engaged in internal struggles to eliminate the racist, sexist, and chauvinist elements within them, and to the extent that they affirm the humanity of others.

This is, of course, a process. Every historical community, including the Jews, has been greatly distorted by the impact of its history of oppression. All of these traditions contain racist or chauvinist elements. But the failure of the ideas of both the melting pot and communist universalism has shown that the attempt to remedy this by transcending or suppressing particularism can also have devastating consequences.

In fact, it is precisely through deeply understanding one's own particular history that one can find a way to identify with others. Every one of us—whether we are Jews, Arabs, Turks, Armenians, WASPs, Chinese, Japanese, Mexicans, Brazilians, Argentinians, English, French, or German—has come from a community whose history is a history of oppression. Those who come from recently oppressed minorities will find it easier to recognize this history of oppression. But even ethnicities that in the past few hundred years have been involved in oppressing others are nevertheless products of earlier histories in which a ruling elite oppressed the majority. The official history of these national groups tends to be the history imposed by the ruling group of oppressors, yet if one digs deeper, one can find cultural clues that may help people remember the suppressed collective history of the oppressed within that society. Sometimes it may take building an imaginative history to uncover these roots (as Jewish women sometimes have to do within Jewish culture in order to rediscover their own suppressed history), but they are there for most people and most national groupings. Most of the human race, including most nations and most ethnic groups, have emerged from a long history of oppression. In rediscovering the truth about oneself and one's history, one can better identify with the pain and suffering of others—and with their struggle to end a world of oppression.

We need to aspire to a transcendent vision that both affirms the particularity of each people and each historical tradition, and yet also articulates a vision of people living in peace and harmony and with mutual respect for one another. If this is one of the transcendent possibilities for the human race, then anti-Semitism stands as one of the impediments to a new world that must be fought for with all our energies. We fight anti-Semitism not because we wish to have the freedom to abandon our Jewishness, but because it is the deepest insight of Judaism that all ways of demeaning human beings ultimately demean the image of the divine, the legacy and reality for all of us. It is precisely to make this antiracist point, say the rabbis, that the Bible talks of the first human being (androgynous—"male and female created He them") as having been formed from the dust of all the earth, to show that all races and divisions derive from the same fundamental reality.

From this interpretation of Judaism, the struggle against racism in all forms is an absolute religious and moral necessity, just as from the standpoint of Jewish self-interest the elimination of racism is a political necessity. And that goal is certainly what we Jews intend when we say, "Next Year in Jerusalem," next year in a world in which all forms of oppression and hatred have been eliminated.

As I argued earlier in this book, Judaism emerged as a revolutionary religion whose message was that the world could be fundamentally changed to one which embodied principles of justice, caring and love. That message provoked so much hostility and anger that the Jewish people themselves have often tried to muzzle or tone it down, recasting their religious consciousness away from its revolutionary meaning to a focus on the rituals which were meant to embody and remind us of the message. Even some who are involved in various contemporary forms of Jewish renewal sometimes try to avoid the confrontational and provocative nature of a God who tells us that we should love our neighbors as ourselves and pursue justice and champion the cause of the oppressed. It is so much easier and acceptable to try to read into our religion a spirituality that exclusively focuses inward than to confront the challenge of a God who asks us to heal, repair, and transform the world (a healing that is outward as well as inward). And staying away from all these social justice crusades makes us so much more acceptable as a people, so much less in conflict with the dominant powers in American society, so much less in conflict with the understandable desire of many Jews to "make it" in this society rather than to challenge the fundamental structures of injustice and alienation. Yet there are many Jews who read the tradition in the way that I do, who understand that Judaism's underlying message is a revolutionary challenge to every form of domination and oppression. It is we, more than any, who are frustrated at the insensitivity of the Left toward Judaism and the Jewish people. I spend a lot of my time challenging the ways that the Jewish community has abandoned what I believe to be the essence of Judaism and has instead allied itself with the materialism, spiritual deadness, narrow-mindedness, moral obtuseness, self-righteousness and one-dimensionality of American society. Yet in trying to convince Jews to reconnect with the revolutionary impulses embodied in the "Jewish liberation" approach that I have learned from the Torah and the Prophets, I find some of the resistance to be based on the bad experience Jews have had with the Left. I find myself having to spend an inordinate amount of time explaining why the ideas make sense even if the Left hasn't done such a good job of embodying them. So my challenge to the Left flows also from my commitment to remain true to Judaism as I understand it— a religion that calls upon us to be partners with God in finishing creation, a religion that tells us that the fundamental power that created the universe created the possibility of transformation toward a moral order. It is when we speak most authentically from our experience as a people and from the religious and cultural heritage that emerged from that experience that we can be most effective allies of the liberal and progressive movements for social change.

Afterword and Afterwards

Nothing feels more demeaning and "uncool" than to ask you to send tax-deductible contributions. But the truth is that we don't have enough support and we need your help. Jewish liberals in the organized Jewish community rarely give us money because they feel angered by our outspoken opposition to Israeli policy on the West Bank and Gaza. Many liberals on the Left and in some liberal foundations see us as "too Jewish," for reasons we've analyzed in this book. So we need your support, donations, subscriptions to the magazine, gift subscriptions for your friends, and help in getting others to buy this book.

I'd be interested in hearing from you personally, to learn about your experiences in relationship to the issues raised in this book, and to learn about what happens as you attempt to introduce these ideas to friends, co-workers, and colleagues in the various social-change movements or liberal and progressive cultural and political circles.

Due to the large volume of mail I receive, I probably will not be able to write back, unless you indicate that you are a *Tikkun* subscriber (and even in those cases, it has sometimes taken as much as six to nine months to respond to personal mail). But I promise to read and think about your letter. Write me at 5100 Leona Street, Oakland, CA 94619.

Being a real ally to us means getting involved with us. We are attempting to create a national organization called the Committee for Judaism and Social Justice—and we'd love to have you become involved in it. You can read the description of what we are trying to do in the addendum that follows this section.

But you can become an active ally in other ways. Subscribe to the magazine and get others to subscribe (mail check for $31 or VISA/Mastercard information to Tikkun, 5100 Leona Street, Oakland, Ca. 94619. By becoming a subscriber you become part of the ongoing community of people who are thinking about and addressing these issues—and it is a community that needs your support.

Most important: Spread these ideas, raise them in conversations with friends and co-workers, write about them, and get others to think about them. Together, we can make a difference.

A "normal" book shows that it obeys the Protestant etiquette by not going beyond "respectable boundaries"—it may advocate an idea, but not give the reader some specific way to become involved. Part of the reason we started Tikkun Books *as a new publishing house was to allow for a specifically Jewish radical voice that does not respect or credit this kind of externally imposed boundary. We want you to become involved in the struggle against anti-Semitism, and we want to provide you with a mechanism for doing so. Hence our description of the Committee for Judaism and Social Justice*

Getting Involved

What is the Committee for Judaism and Social Justice?

We are a nationwide organization of progressive Jews who want to live in a society that embodies Judaism's commandments to pursue justice and to love our neighbors as ourselves. We operate as the education and outreach arm of *Tikkun* magazine. While *Tikkun* presents a variety of perspectives on many questions, it also has a fundamental outlook about how to change the world.

In order to make changes in the larger world, however, we must first try to change the Jewish world and the world of liberal and progressive politics. The Jewish world needs to make a deeper commitment to progressive values, and the liberal and progressive social-change movements need to develop a sensitivity to people's psychological, ethical, and spiritual concerns, as well as a new commitment to the legitimate needs and interests of the Jewish people. We are a nationwide network of activists who will assist one another in these tasks in the years ahead.

We have no illusions that these tasks will be accomplished easily in the next decades—this is a struggle that will continue throughout our lives. But we also know that in ten or twenty years, the connections and alliances we have built through the *Tikkun*-CJSJ network will enable us to be more effective agents of social change. Many of us are professionals of various sorts, and we will use the social power we have in our personal and working lives as levers to gain influence within the organized Jewish community and the liberal and progressive social-change movements. But to be effective, we need to be part of a larger community of social change that has shared values and a shared vision of a better world. We are building that community and that vision in CJSJ. A central part of our activism is study—of *Tikkun*'s rich, informative, and provocative articles, and of Jewish texts and Jewish history. At conferences and other arenas for exchanging and refining our thinking, we will improve our ability to be activists in the larger world.

Why Do We Want To Change the Jewish World?

The organized Jewish communities in the U.S. and Canada have long been dominated by conservative forces. These communities are not organized democratically, and those who speak in the name of American and Canadian Jews are usually not elected by or accountable to those in whose name they claim to speak. Power in the Jewish world resides primarily with those who have the most money, assisted by a large array of professionals whose primary skill is to raise funds or to show those with money that their interests will be served. The traditional Jewish respect for scholars and intellectuals has largely been obliterated in North America; at best it has been relegated to religious yeshivot or tame, dispassionate Jewish studies arenas in universities. The mainstream of American-Jewish life has become increasingly anti-intellectual, antispiritual, undemocratic, stifling to creativity and change, and materialistic. Organized around self-interest and often insensitive to the needs of others, the Jewish world often reflects the same selfishness and self-centeredness that is the hallmark of contemporary Western society.

It wasn't always this way. American Jews used to be at the forefront of battles for social justice and equality. But in the past decades a fearfulness of the "other"—whether it be African Americans, Palestinians, or non-Jews in general—has infused American-Jewish life with paranoia and insensitivity.

Many of the most sensitive young Jews, those who take intellectual, spiritual, ethical, and social-action concerns seriously, look elsewhere to meet their needs, having grown up in a Jewish world that seemed to have little to offer them. They don't take much interest in Judaism because they identify it with the stultifying and boring experiences they had in Hebrew school or in their first encounters with the organized Jewish community.

We seek a different kind of Jewish community—one passionately committed to Jewish ethical and spiritual values. The central principles we seek to establish in that community are:

Justice, Justice Shalt Thou Pursue. Judaism is not just about self-interest. It is about remaking the world in a fair and just way. This is not just a set of pretty words to be repeated in religious services or in pious speeches, but a political agenda that demands that we:

- eliminate poverty, homelessness, and hunger for all the peoples of the world. This involves redistributing the world's resources and productive capacities to ensure that all people are recognized as created equally in God's image, and hence equally entitled to share in the benefits, as well as the costs, of living on this planet;
- combat all forms of oppression, including those based on sexism and heterosexism, racism, ageism, national and religious chauvinism, and economic inequality;
- democratize the economic and political institutions of society and introduce broad-based citizen participation in the major decisions on production, the use of resources, and the division of labor;

- equalize power and extend respect for women at every level—including all the institutions of Jewish life. This must involve reclaiming women's experience and women's history, and reworking Jewish religious life to incorporate the insights and concerns of women;
- heal the damage that has been done to the planet by economic systems that encourage wasteful production, profligate consumption, and disregard for the future. Our obligation as stewards of the earth requires that we support a rational plan to use the earth's scarce resources and productive capacities in ways that are fair to all and sensitive to the environment. Individual awareness is a necessary but insufficient condition for saving the planet. We also need to create a world in which ecologically sound decisions are rewarded, rather than regarded as individual acts of moral sensitivity.

When you come into your land, do not oppress the stranger. Remember that you were strangers in the land of Egypt. We are strong supporters of the State of Israel. Some of us will go to live in Israel, others will build strong ties between American Jews and Israelis. We believe that Israel is necessary for the survival of the Jewish people.

However, we reject the State of Israel's current policies concerning Palestinians and its own Arab minority. We believe the Palestinian people have the same right to national self-determination that we, the Jewish people, rightly sought for ourselves when we created the State of Israel. For that reason, we support the creation of a demilitarized Palestinian state in the West Bank and Gaza Strip. We support the right of Palestinians to choose their own leadership democratically and to determine their own fate. Yet we also want to ensure Israel's safety and security—so we support all military and diplomatic steps necessary to ensure Israel's survival against hostile foes. Ultimately, however, we believe that Israel's greatest security lies in making peace with its neighbors. To achieve this peace, Israel must ensure the same opportunities and respect for its Arab minority (those who elect to stay in Israel after the creation of a Palestinian state) that Jews rightfully seek for themselves as a minority in the United States.

We also support those in Israel who seek greater economic, social, and political equality for Oriental Jews (Sephardim/Mizrachim), who are disproportionately represented among the poor; Jews from Ethiopia; and Jews from the Soviet Union. These Jews, too, have become "strangers" in our midst.

Love Your Neighbor as Yourself. This principle must become a central reality for anyone who is involved in Judaism, not just a pretty phrase to be invoked on ceremonial occasions. Love of one's neighbors must include direct caring for Jews—hands-on aid to the poor, the sick, the elderly, and the emotionally and spiritually needy—as well as philanthropic contributions. Some Jews have already organized "tzedaka collectives," groups that work together to deliver services personally, like feeding the hungry, providing child care, assisting the elderly in shopping and other chores, visiting the sick, repairing damaged or deteriorated housing. We envision a Jewish community in which this kind of hands-on work is the norm, with each person dedicating several hours a month to some kind of personal charity, in addition to undertaking the traditional, passive act of donating money.

But love of one's neighbors must mean not only caring for Jews—our community must be concerned for others as well. We must expend community resources in the struggle against racism and poverty. To the extent that Jews have achieved economic success, our commitment to love of our neighbors requires that we be willing to struggle for social programs, even if they entail increasing the tax burden on ourselves and other groups who are doing well financially. Caring for others is not just a matter of individual acts of kindness, concern, or volunteerism—it is also a willingness to support those societal changes and economic sacrifices that can enable others to share equally in access to health care, employment, housing, food, and other basic goods and services that are now distributed inequitably.

Other ethnic and national communities must begin to see Jews as allies rather than adversaries in these struggles. Throughout the past 150 years, Jews have had a disproportionate presence in social-change organizations, but mostly as individuals who rarely paid serious attention to their Jewishness and how it informed their struggles to achieve social change. But for other ethnic and national communities to regard us as allies, Jews must be part of these struggles as Jews, affirming our own history and tradition and our commitment to Israel and the Jewish people even as we work for larger social transformation. This goal cannot be accomplished by a few "community relations" experts visiting the leaderships of other communities. Rather, it must be the product of a conscious campaign by grassroots Jewish organizations to involve themselves in the daily struggles and concerns of others.

Sensitivity to others—their traditions and their economic and social oppressions—must become an integral part of Jewish education. If Jews no longer had to leave the Jewish community in order to care for others, many more of our young people would remain committed to Judaism and the Jewish people.

We also seek to heal the deep pain that we, as Jews, still feel from the accumulated psychological legacy of thousands of years of oppression. Jews have every right to feel anger at non-Jews for the ways we have been abandoned and oppressed. But while we validate our anger and pain, our goal is to move beyond these feelings to a new relationship with non-Jews based on mutual respect. It is in the true self-interest of Jews to move beyond the "goyim-bashing" that has sometimes characterized Jewish communities since the Holocaust. Many non-Jews share little responsibility for what happened to us in the past, but some Jews' paranoid fear of the other and certainty that non-Jews will betray us again can become self-fulfilling prophecies. Of course, healing our pain does not mean ignoring the real dangers and enemies of the Jewish people—there still are those who hate Jews irrationally, and we are committed to fighting them in every arena, at every opportunity.

It is particularly important to us to heal the rift between African

Americans and Jews. The pain and oppression of African Americans are psychically marginalized by the dominant white majority, just as Jewish pain and oppression was marginalized in European society. African Americans here, like Jews in European and Islamic societies, are the most economically oppressed, feared, and despised sector of society.

Jews did not create this situation, but like all other groups, we benefit to some extent from social and economic structures that guarantee that when times get tough, the hardships will fall disproportionately on another ethnic group. African Americans sometimes respond to Jews as though we control these structures (we don't) or as though we were the only white group they were willing to confront seriously. Often the attacks on Jews are unfair, linked with anti-Semitism, and generate legitimate Jewish resentment and anger. We deplore anti-Semitism among African Americans and all peoples of color: We understand their rage at oppression, but we are not willing to become scapegoats of that rage. Racism or tyranny by the oppressed is understandable, but not something we will tolerate. But neither will we allow the anti-Semitism of some of the oppressed to keep us from struggling to change the social order that generates this irrational response. Nor will we pretend that Jews are innocent victims: We are part of a larger economic system that has been oppressive to people of color, we benefit from that system, and to the extent that our community participates in it without being actively involved in the struggle to change it, we deserve some part of the blame.

In the emerging multicultural world of the twenty-first century, self-interest requires other-interest. The Jewish community should be restructured to reflect that awareness and concern. Not merely self-interest, but also a commitment to Jewish values, lead us to insist that Jews build a community that is other-oriented, that recognizes love of one's neighbor as a central Jewish value and virtue.

A note on our Jewishness. CJSJ is composed of secular Jews and religious Jews of every persuasion. We do not expect or require of our members any particular commitment to Judaism or Jewish practice. However, Judaism occupies a privileged position in our work in two respects:

1. We recognize that the creative energies of the Jewish people were expressed throughout most of history through our religious language, customs, literature, and philosophy. So we, too, draw upon Judaism and Torah for inspiration and insights, and try to transcend the knee-jerk, antireligious idioms of previous stages of liberalism, in which the desire to escape the powerful patriarchal and authoritarian tendencies within Judaism led some people to discard it entirely.

2. We understand that movements for social change rarely survive unless they are embedded in a rich system of customs, ceremonies, and traditions. Since Judaism is one such system—developed by the Jewish people in

their struggle to liberate themselves from slavery and to bring to the world a message of transformation—we embrace many of the liberatory forms of Judaism as our own. At the same time, we are aware of the ways that Judaism has in the past incorporated patriarchal and authoritarian practices, and we support efforts to update Judaism's fundamentally liberatory message by unequivocally identifying with the struggle for women's liberation and the attempt to purge Judaism of patriarchal practices. For some of us, this is a struggle within a religious (or halachic) tradition; for others, it is merely the necessary adaptation of a rich but continually evolving cultural tradition. In either case, we affirm the value of studying the tradition and its literature, even as we engage in the traditional Jewish activity of reunderstanding and transforming it.

With this in mind, we describe ourselves as a Committee for Judaism and Social Justice—not implying that we are a religious organization, but that we are deeply committed to the wisdom within Judaism, Torah, and Jewish observance. We also explicitly wish to affirm the contributions that the secular Yiddish, socialist, Bundist, and Zionist movements have made to the collective wisdom and understanding of the Jewish people, just as we are proud to incorporate the new insights from Jewish feminist and gay and lesbian movements. We refer to these as well when we talk about Judaism.

Why do we Want to Rethink the Fundamental Assumptions of Liberal and Progressive Social-Change Movements?

There are two ways that the Left has been misguided. Although the goals of liberal and progressive movements are admirable, many of these movements ignore basic psychological, ethical, and spiritual needs. They also wilfully ignore the needs and struggles of Jews—and have sometimes collaborated with anti-Semitism. We want to educate the Left on both issues.

Liberal and progressive social-change movements have been correct to define a set of struggles for economic entitlements and political rights. Yet for most people in the West, the primary form of oppression is not economic deprivation or the denial of political rights. Rather, it is the deprivation of meaning. Human beings have fundamental needs for meaning in their work, love, and communities. The fundamental crisis of advanced capitalist society lies in the way it systematically prevents the fulfillment of these needs. But the Left exhibits no understanding of these issues, and instead focuses solely on economic and social equality. CJSJ's goal is to launch a **Campaign for A Politics of Meaning** that helps the various social-change movements to rethink the dominant paradigm for progressive politics.

Work. People need ethically meaningful work that enables them to use their intelligence and creativity and to cooperate and care for others. But the competitive marketplace has shaped work around the needs of capital and the requisites of large, undemocratic bureaucracies. Most people are forced to deny an important part of who they are in order to function in the world of work. Eventually, who they are changes to fit the "reality" of the competitive marketplace.

Under such conditions, work is often stressful and unfulfilling. Many people deny to themselves that they could have a different kind of life—they come to believe that this is "just how it is in the real world" and that to want anything else would be unrealistic or utopian. As they accommodate themselves to this stressful reality, they become deadened and less capable of being intelligent and creative. They also become susceptible to a variety of health problems. Research on stress shows that even when people are unaware of their powerlessness and frustration, these factors nevertheless correlate directly with heart disease, cancer, and other life-threatening illnesses.

Yet even when people recognize that their jobs are alienating, they often blame themselves. Long-conditioned to accept the dominant capitalist ideology that "you can make it if you really try," they come to believe it is their own fault that they don't have more fulfilling jobs. ("If only I had been smarter, worked harder, been more beautiful or charming," they believe, "I would have found more fulfilling work.") One finds this self-blaming attitude up and down the economic ladder, often held as tenaciously by stockbrokers, scientists, corporate lawyers, or government bureaucrats as by hospital workers, hotel employees, or assembly-line workers. People blame themselves rather than recognize that the whole system has frustrated their ability to find morally meaningful and personally fulfilling work. The anger they suppress at work becomes internalized as self-blame, and in this form, it plays a large unconscious role in disrupting their loving relationships.

Of course, work has been oppressive for most people throughout history. In precapitalist societies, feudal or slave-owning ruling classes justified this oppression through a series of ideologies based on "natural hierarchies." Each person had a station in life, allocated and fixed from birth, and held in place by the power of the ruling class and its armies. The capitalist order promised to break this system of social subordination and offered the possibility of individual advance. But in the nineteenth century, and to some extent through the period of the New Deal, large numbers of workers understood that there was another barrier—class structure—which they needed to overcome. Work may have been as oppressive as before, but people who had this new "class consciousness" stopped blaming themselves for their oppression. What is unique about the organization of work in the past fifty years is the degree to which an understanding of the barriers of class structure has faded from popular consciousness and been replaced by the model of meritocracy—the idea that someone can always make it if he or she is "good enough"—with a corresponding escalation of individual self-blame and the attendant psychological and physical consequences. This self-blame makes it difficult for people to feel that they have the right to a workplace that allows them the opportunity to use their fundamental human capacities. Instead, people withdraw into the hope that in private life they will obtain the satisfactions not available in the world of work.

Yet the self-blame does not magically disappear when people leave the workplace—the psychodynamics of work are often brought home. The pain can be so great that some try to deaden themselves by abusing alcohol or drugs, or by over-engaging in otherwise healthful activities (e.g., exercise, political or religious activities, even socializing or being sexually active) to bury the memories and pains of work. Others quickly abandon the memory of work, but because they have tried so hard to bury their pain, they are inaccessible to their intimate partners. And the buried angers always flare up, usually in arguments, constant depressive states, or seemingly baseless edginess and tension, which further interfere with loving relationships.

Even people whose jobs give them much greater freedom, such as lawyers, doctors, psychologists, writers, professors, and some scientists and engineers, find that work takes a dramatic toll. To be successful, one increasingly must not only sell a skill, but sell oneself. Those who do best in the competitive marketplace have learned to objectify others, treat people as commodities, and become the kind of person who will "sell." The narcissistic personalities that emerge as a result are perfect manipulators—and greatly rewarded in the world of work. But when they return to the personal sphere, they are unable to treat others as anything but objects to be manipulated, and this makes them very poor candidates for loving relationships.

Love. Because of the experiences in the world of work, loving and trusting relationships become increasingly difficult. The media has focused much attention on problems in families, but the same problems exist in friendships, which are also in crisis today. Friendships increasingly lose their sustaining character as major supports for people, and instead become instrumental means to an end—to get contacts, clients, jobs, or other forms of help for the future—and not to provide safe and committed relationships. Loving relationships are similarly undermined, and there is increasing social sanction for the separation of sexuality from love, caring, and commitment. More and more, one finds it easier to get sex than emotional security. Younger people sometimes scoff at the need for emotional security or commitment, believing that there will be an endless supply of people to love. This belief reflects the "common sense" of the capitalist market, which has taught us to think of one another as items of consumption that can easily be discarded when some tension or problem arises in a relationship. This supermarket of relationships leads people to use and abuse one another, all under the guise of exercising freedom and gathering experiences. In the long run, its effect is to convince people that they really can't trust anyone, thereby reinforcing the "look after number one because no one else is going to" mentality of the capitalist market.

Community. Relationships used to be embedded in larger communities of meaning and purpose that gave contexts to individual relationships and families. Whether it was being part of a people (such as the Jewish community), a political movement, or a union, these larger frameworks provided a sense of shared meaning and direction. But the logic of the capitalist marketplace undermines those larger communities, insisting that the only "real" thing is self-interest, and that any larger goals or meanings are simply projections of personal needs. As the larger communities are undermined by the logic of self-interest, each individual family or relationship is suddenly forced to face the world on its own. Instead of being embedded in a larger frame of meaning, each relationship must now be the meaning of life for those who are in it. That is too much for most human relationships—they are asked to carry too much meaning, and end up carrying too little. And because of the marketplace in relationships, people feel free to search elsewhere once their own relationship falls short of their fantasies.

Leisure. Faced with this crisis of meaning, people are encouraged to imagine that there should be some special area of life in which real fulfillment might take place—leisure time, either after work or during retirement. Art, culture, and play are consigned to this special arena, rather than integrated into the total fabric of our lives. We are told that competition with other advanced capitalist societies makes it "unrealistic" to expect much time to be given to these leisure-time activities.

From our standpoint, this focus is doubly mistaken. First, we challenge the argument's hidden premise that the goal of societal organization is to maximize society's abilities to produce material goods. Counter to that, we believe that the highest goal of a society is to maximize people's possibilities to actualize their creative capacities, including their abilities to be loving, creative, cooperative, and engaged in activities that increase their intellectual, moral, and spiritual well-being. Material well-being is only one way to facilitate these possibilities, and must not be used as the definitive criterion of how well a society is doing. Given this definition of goals, it is unrealistic for a society not to give enough time to leisure activities and still expect to be efficient at achieving these ends.

Second, we question the assumption that art, culture, and play should be divorced from work. Human beings may be more productive and effective workers—even in narrow economic terms—when the workplace itself integrates time and space for art, culture, and play. But today, access to these activities can only be "bought" in leisure time, usually by those with considerable financial resources. The rest of us—and sometimes even the well-to-do—feel frustrated and deprived in the world of work. Yet we interpret this frustration as an unrealistic desire on our part, and to the extent that we can envision little time in our lives to meet our needs, we feel angry at ourselves for having failed to be more successful and hence able to buy more leisure time.

The result of these dynamics is that people are in great pain in personal life. They feel adrift, worried that their most intimate relationships may fall apart, or unable to make them work in ways that provide real intimacy. They blame themselves, feel terrible about their pain, and then try to hide from themselves what they think they know: that they have made failures of their lives. Because of this self-blame, they are unable to talk honestly to others about their pain. Instead, they often pretend that everything is won derful, because if it weren't, they would have no one to blame but themselves. The Right has helped these people find external forces to blame—gays, uppity women, African Americans, Jews, Iraqis, communists, terrorists, drug traders, or some "other" on whom they can project their anger. By addressing pain in this way, the Right helps make people feel better by reducing self-blame. The Left, because it ignores these central issues, actually reinforces the individual "take responsibility" model that increases people's pain.

CJSJ strives for a liberal and progressive politics that talks about these critical issues. Such a politics must insist that healing the deprivation of meaning be central to the social-change agenda—and it must develop ways to address these deprivations in daily life. For example, we should switch our political focus from how to achieve individual rights to what kinds of societal changes are necessary to create a society that is safe for love and intimacy, and that promotes ethical and spiritual sensitivity.

This focus distinguishes us from other organizations that also do valuable work. Americans for Peace Now, for example, shares our critique of Israeli policy, but does not enter into issues concerning societal change. New Jewish Agenda, in a radical form, and the American Jewish Congress, in a liberal form, both focus on the traditional liberal/left struggle for rights and economic entitlements. But neither concerns itself with the deprivation of meaning in contemporary society. While we support the work of these organizations, we believe that they illustrate the way in which the Left, and the Jewish Left, has failed to address the central psychological, spiritual, and ethical needs of most people. This failure has rendered the Left powerless to deliver the also important economic and political gains it supports.

The liberal and progressive movements have also been remiss in addressing the concerns and needs of the Jewish people. Jews have been one of the most oppressed groups in history, and have played a central role in developing theories of human liberation. Jews have developed a series of strategies to avoid being marginalized that range from assimilation to Zionism to a form of internationalism that denies Jewish particularism. It is this last tendency that dominates the American Left. Too often Jews feel they need to show that they are not narrowly particularistic, so they ignore anti-Semitism (when it is articulated by other oppressed groups), or disassociate themselves from the demands for Jewish liberation.

We intend to play a different role in the liberal and progressive communities. We will insist on the legitimacy of Israel, of the Jewish national liberation struggle, and of the need for non-Jews to address and deal consciously with their anti-Semitism. Just as women openly confronted sexism within the Left, we intend to confront anti-Semitism openly. That also means confronting the internalized anti-Semitism of many Jews on the Left. Many Jews are unaware of the ways they act to reassure their non-Jewish friends that they are not "too Jewish," that they can look and talk like non-Jews, adopt the right mannerisms, and show how little they care about "narrowly" Jewish concerns. We believe, by contrast, that it is precisely this attempt to portray ourselves as "above" particularistic concerns—which every other community has—that makes us suspect. Rather, as Jews we want to insist that the Left be as committed to our concerns and struggles as it is to those of any other group—just as we insist in the Jewish world that Jews transcend their particularistic concerns to be involved in the liberation of others.

Starting CJSJ

Although I've written this section as though CJSJ was already a functioning reality, the truth is that in the Spring of 1992 we are just a group of people spread around the U.S. and Canada and England and Australia and Israel who share these values and share a vision of building this kind of organization. The ideas articulated here represent the vision of what this organization intends to be.

We are not seeking to create a "mass organization"—we are seeking a small cadre of people who are committed to the vision articulated here. CJSJ members will become an ongoing support group for each other in the decades ahead, helping each other to advance into positions of influence and power in both the world of secular liberal and progressive politics and in the Jewish world. Sharing a common perspective, meeting with each other from time to time to discuss our experiences as we attempt to actualize the CJSJ vision, we will be able to learn from each other's successes and analyze what we have tried that has not been quite so successful. But CJSJ is not meant to be a narrowly defined "political group"—it is also and importantly a structure of human caring and mutual support. We will be concerned with each other's careers and families, our ability to find pleasure and happiness and fulfillment—recognizing that an important element in the physical and psychological wellbeing of all of us is extent to which we feel ourselves part of a community of people who really care about each other. While a national cadre organization cannot substitute for a family or a local community, it can provide a network of people who really care about each other and who, through the years, grow closer and more committed to each other. For that very reason, we are not throwing CJSJ open to everyone who wants to be a part of it, but rather only to those who really share the vision and the politics and who feel comfortable with what we've been doing in Tikkun magazine. What we hope is to create a community of people who share *both* the politics in general and the willingness to commit to each other and the project of CJSJ in particular.

Though there are groups of people involved with CJSJ who are already doing work in various areas, supporting the Israeli peace movement or opposing domestic racism or spreading ideas from our Campaign for a

Politics of Meaning or actively challenging anti-Semitism on the Left, and although there have already been some chapters created and many groups of people meeting in "study groups," the fact is that CJSJ remains more of an idea than a functioning reality. If you've read and been turned on by this book and by the vision articulated here about CJSJ, perhaps you can join us and help make CJSJ more real.

If you want to work with us, there are several things you can do. You can create a small group of people in your own area who get together on a regular basis and discuss *The Socialism of Fools,* discuss the *Tikkun Anthology,* discuss *Surplus Powerlessness,* discuss current articles in *Tikkun* magazine, and discuss this founding statement of CJSJ. When you get some subsection of them who feel that they understand and are in substantive agreement with the CJSJ position as articulated here, they can become a local CJSJ chapter.

Or you can become involved in our ongoing Campaign for a Politics of Meaning—our attempt to shift the way liberals and progressives think about politics. Or you can become involved in our campaign in the Jewish world. Write to us and we'll tell you what plans we have about these.

We are also organizing a nationwide Students for Judaism and Social Justice (SJSJ) for young people under thirty. Chapters have already formed on several West Coast campuses and we plan to sponsor national conferences as well.

Each year there is a national gathering of activists in CJSJ and SJSJ.

If you want to be one of the people involved in creating CJSJ or SJSJ, please write to us: CJSJ (or SJSJ), 5100 Leona Street, Oakland, Ca. 94619. Tell us about yourself, what parts of the analysis most excite you, what skills or resources you might bring to the organization, and what direction you'd like to focus your energy and talents on in the next few years.

Please understand, however, that there is no paid staff for this organization. Nor is there any funding base to hire organizers or even secretarial staff. If you know people who want to volunteer time or become interns with us, please have them contact us. But in the meantime, if it takes us time to get back to you, have patience. Meanwhile, the key is to take the ideas, circulate them, get others to think about them, and create local discussions about them. Don't wait for us to do that!

Tikkun Books

The Socialism of Fools is the second in a series of books being published by the new Jewish renewal publishing house—*Tikkun* Books. The first book is the *Tikkun Anthology* (1992)—a collection of articles from the magazine including essays, poetry, and fiction by Woody Allen, Allen Ginsberg, Cornel West, Jessica Benjamin, Annie Dillard, Peter Gabel, Marge Piercy, Rachel Adler, Daniel Landes, Todd Gitlin, Carol Gilligan, Geoffrey Hartman, Michael Walzer, David Biale, and Arthur Waskow.

The *Tikkun Anthology* can be ordered directly by sending a check for $19.85 (paperback) or $42.85 (hardback) to Tikkun Books, 5100 Leona Street, Oakland, Ca. 94619. You can also order *The Socialism of Fools* personally or as a gift for a friend or family member directly by sending $11.70 to Tikkun Books, 5100 Leona Street, Oakland, Ca. 94619. All prices include postage. (If you order ten or more, the cost is $8.95 per copy including postage.)

Bookstores can order both these books through Publisher's Group West at (800) 788-3123.